D1233819

Pennsylvania Fireside Tales
Volume III

(Origins & Foundations of Old-time Pennsylvania Mountain Legends & Folktales)

By Jeffrey R. Frazier
Author of:
Pennsylvania Fireside Tales
And
The Black Ghost of Scotia
& More Pennsylvania Fireside Tales

Tell me a tale of the timber lands,
  And the old time pioneers;
Somethin' a poor man understands,
  With his feelings as well as his ears,

Tell of the old log house – about
  The loft, the puncheon floor –
The fireplace with crane swinging out
  And the latchstring through the door.

James Whitcomb Riley

Pennsylvania Fireside Tales
Volume III

By Jeffrey R. Frazier

Copyright 1999 by Jeffrey R. Frazier
Egg Hill Publications
143 Cedar Ridge Drive
Port Matilda, Pa., 16870

Second Printing, June, 2000
Printed in the United States of America
Jostens Commercial Publications
 401 Science Park Road
 State College, Penna. 16803

All photos by the author, unless otherwise noted.

ISBN 0-9652351-2-2

Cover:
Sentinel Rock,
Michaux State Forest, Franklin County
Drawing by James J. Frazier based on an old news photo.

Previous Page:
Head of the large stag shot by Samuel Strohecker in
High Valley, Centre County, 1898. (Drawing by James
Frazier – based on an old photograph).

To my parents and to both my grandmothers,

From whom I learned to love the Pennsylvania mountains
and the old-time mountain folks whose stories
form the soul of these awe-inspiring hills.

Table of Contents

LIST OF PHOTOS

INTRODUCTION

Back in 1991, when I started to organize and write the episodes for the first volume in my *Pennsylvania Fireside Tales* series, I decided I could no longer afford the time it would take to travel and collect any more stories. I needed time to write if I was ever going to produce even just one book, and so I resolved to stop searching for the old tales in the quaint, out-of-the-way, spots that seemed to keep pulling me away from my self-appointed task. However, it seems I just can't resist a good story, and whenever a promising "lead" came up, I chased it down. As a result, I've collected, and am still collecting, some of the best material I've ever found

Not all the blame for my inability to stop collecting good material should fall upon the fascinating folk tales of Pennsylvania. Probably just as much fault has to be placed upon the mountains themselves. Somehow they've always drawn me into their cool depths and shaded solitude, charming me with a seemingly endless treasure store of wonderful sights and comforting breezes. Whenever I need to feel at peace with myself or with the world, or whenever the pressures of the workplace or the daily "grind" of everyday life seem to be overwhelming, I can lose myself in the mountains, and there feel alive once more.

These grand and somber ridges will, I suspect, always be a source of strength for me, just as they have been for many others over the years.

In fact, it would not be an exaggeration to say that if anyone wishes to experience one of those rare moments of true happiness that occurs in a lifetime, they should go to the mountains and search for a teller of the old tales. When sitting amidst the scenery that is woven into the heart and soul of the stories themselves, cares of this present hectic age seem to melt away, and the listener is indeed transported to another level – a finer "phase" of existence that everyone should be able to experience whenever they so desire. It has been this writer's privilege to feel a renewed optimism each time I've gone back to the hills, and that's the same "high" that I hope the reader gets when he peruses the stories preserved in the *Fireside Tales* series.

Many folks have indeed told me how much they've enjoyed the anecdotes I've brought to the attention of the general public, and others have even thanked me for doing so. I've always felt these episodes deserve more publicity then they've gotten in the past, and positive comments from many kind readers have reinforced that belief. Certainly folklorists and scholars in related fields have collected these types of tales over the years, but the results of their efforts usually don't get widely disseminated. In fact, it would seem the scholars' main objective is to dissect, categorize, and hoard the stories for their own enjoyment, oftentimes seemingly looking down with disdain upon anyone else who dares to consider folktales as property of the "folk" where they originated in the first place. Call it a "popularizer" versus a "protectionist" philosophy, but, to me, once a folktale has been cast into an "ivory tower" of learning and placed upon some dry page of a scholar's notebook, it loses its charm and its attraction for the average person, becoming a desiccated and lifeless object.

That's not to say, on the other hand, that a legend or folktale should be meddled with in any way by the non-scholar once he's collected it. These survivors of an earlier time should not be embellished, polished, or trifled with if their purity is to be maintained, their window on the past to remain unclouded. It is this approach that I've tried to take in deciding how to preserve the annals in the *Fireside Tales* volumes. I've also tried to maintain the same care when discussing the history behind the tales, but intentions do exceed actions at times, despite the best attempts to insure otherwise.

I was suddenly reminded of this last fact one afternoon last year when I was having a book signing at Homan's Store in Potter Mills, Centre County. Located at the entrance to the Seven Mountains country of Mifflin and Centre Counties, the little store is a unique throwback to an earlier and less-hurried time, and is a favorite stopping place for hunters and hikers who need to stock up on groceries or refuel their trucks before driving off onto one of the many dirt mountain roads nearby. I always enjoy the atmosphere of the quaint store, but that particular afternoon during the book signing I was enjoying it even more. In talking to the many people who stopped by to have their books autographed, I signed a book for one young gentleman who then asked me where I had gotten the name "Henry Pickett" as the name of the Confederate general who I mention in my story called "Sounds of Battle" in volume I.

Right away I knew I was in trouble. I looked at the story and, sure enough, I had misnamed General George E. Pickett whose name is forever linked to Pickett's charge – the turning point of the Battle of Gettysburg. Since I knew his correct name, the misnaming had been a "slip of the pen", but such mistakes cast doubt on the other historical facts I've tried to weave into the stories, and that's not something I want to happen.

Even though I'm not trained as an historian, I do know something about research methods. Consequently, I do try to avoid mistakes and try also to note when my sources of information may be suspect. Time, however, is always an enemy of accuracy, particularly when you can't devote as much effort as you'd like in researching facts or when you're trying to write after a particularly tiring day at the office.

This dilemma was brought to my attention again when I was at another book signing and a woman told me her parents live in The Scotia Barrens, near State College. She went on to say they live near the flat stone marking the gravesite of

Bert Delige, the infamous murderer whose story "The Black Ghost of Scotia", appears in Volume II. In that story I mention that the flat stone marking the gravesite is no longer there. I did not have the time to verify this fact, but instead relied upon statements in a newspaper article written some twenty years ago.

It is indeed unfortunate that I didn't, and don't, have the proper time to devote to this activity, because it certainly cries out for attention. I'd like nothing better than to just collect and write these tales. However, no one else seems to have the same enthusiasm, or time either, for that matter, and so I continue to do so, imperfect as the results may be now and then. I can only ask the reader to overlook the faults and enjoy the annals, promising to be as historically accurate as I possibly can be in all future efforts. Hopefully the results, though not of the quality that scholars would demand, will still take you to that "higher phase" where you, too, can forget your cares and savor the finer aspects of our Pennsylvania mountains; the majestic peaks that some would say are among the Creator's most masterful works.

RED PANTHER

Pennsylvania's natural underground system of limestone caves has been described as a "honeycomb" of interconnecting passages and cool subterranean streams. The most spectacular of these caverns have often been commercialized and opened to the public for tours, but there are numerous "wild" caves, sometimes even more spectacular than their commercialized counterparts, which also offer many geological wonders and delights to weekend cave explorers. Those "spelunkers" who have explored Madisonburg's Veiled Lady Cave, in Centre County, for example, will remember the seemingly bottomless chasm in one of the side passages that leads to a hidden lake. A small footlog allows an explorer to cross the chasm, but the experience is not for the faint of heart. There is one other wild cave in Centre County that provided another form of breathtaking excitement to a party of Boy Scouts about thirty-five years ago. Located near the town of Centre Hall, McClanahan's cave is known for some interesting flowstone formations, but the discovery of a padlocked box in a side room of the cavern created the most excitement, at least for a few minutes.

The box was empty, it had no bottom either, but the thrill of the discovery will always be remembered by those of us who were there in the cave. We all speculated about what had been stored in the container in the olden times, but the carton was probably nothing more then a remnant of the days when settlers of the area had used McClanahan's Cave for cold storage of their milk and other perishables. On the other hand, the mysterious old crate did reinforce the fact that both commercialized and wild caves have their own separate history and legends.

Not too far away, for example, is the famous Centre County cavern called Penn's Cave. This large commercial attraction is also known as the "all water" cavern because the only way through it is by boat. However, Penn's Cave is also famous for Princess Nittany (for whom Nittany Mountain and Penn State's Nittany Lions are said to be named) and her white lover, who legend claims was drowned in the cave by Nittany's seven brothers. Further west at Indian Caverns, Huntingdon County, a tale is told of "Robber Lewis" and the cache of gold he hid somewhere near that cave. To the east, in Dauphin County, guides at the cavern known as Indian Echo Cave relate the woeful history of Amos Wilson, also known as the "Pennsylvania Hermit". Similarly, at Woodward Cave in Centre County, visitors can hear the legend of Red Panther, a man whose fate was even worse than that of Amos Wilson.

The authenticity of Penn's Cave's legend has been questioned since its source was Henry W. Shoemaker, that well-known embellisher and inventor of such tales. Shoemaker also published the Red Panther legend, but no one has ever seriously investigated whether or not the story could have a factual basis. Many students of such things have assumed that Shoemaker must have invented the story since he published it in his romanticized style. However, the facts seem to suggest that the legend, which survived by staying afloat on the currents of oral history, was around long before Shoemaker ever began writing his books. In fact, if anyone today wants to hear the version of the story the way it was probably told to Shoemaker, then they should travel to the small mountain town of Woodward, and listen to a local person relate the legend the way they heard it from their parents or grandparents, who, in turn, had heard it from theirs. Ray Stover was one such man. He knew the cave's legends well, because he grew up with the place, and had worked there all his life.

"My dad, Braid, when they opened the cave here in 1926, because he was a farmer then, why, he was glad for a little extra work, you know," recalled seventy-seven year old Stover in 1989. "During the winter months he helped clean out the cave. So I've been around the cave all my life actually. My first job was tying on bumper strips. At that time we didn't paste them on, we tied them on with string. I was here when Luther Weaver and Oliver Hosterman went together and opened the cave.

"When I was a kid I had heard some of the Red Panther legend from my father. Later on, over the years, I picked a little more of this up. Somebody, I believe Lute Weaver, he gave me a history of Haines Township. That goes way back, you know, to the Indians. I read some of that. That's where I heard about Red Panther being the son of the chief, and about the Indians inhabiting the cave. Now we knew it as Red Panther's Cave, and it stated it was close by here in Haines Township. So this is the only cave that we knew of at that time. My dad was saying, 'It must be the cave up here because there's no other cave close by except Penn's Cave.' And it was open already, Penn's Cave, and they never said anything about Red Panther.

"But, as I told you, this legend about Red Panther, this is the way I heard it from Mister Weaver; it was in the history of Haines Township somewhat. Red Panther, according to the history, rebelled against the beliefs of the Seneca Indians. The Senecas believed that the beech tree was sacred, and there was an awful lot of beech trees around here at one time. There's one right out here yet, and the other one broke down just about three years ago. And that spites me because when I was fourteen years old I put my name on the side of that beech tree with a pocket knife. Three years ago that beech broke down, and it split right through where I had my name on, so that's gone. I could've showed you that yet. I put my name on there in the year 1929, and there was a lot of beech trees.

"The Seneca Indians here used to gather under beech trees during the thunder storms because they said the beech

4

tree was sacred and lightning would never strike a beech tree. Red Panther told them that he didn't believe in that. In fact, I've never heard of lightning hitting a beech tree either, never. So Red Panther didn't believe in that. He rebelled, and one day he takes an axe and goes out here and starts cutting down a beech tree. And in the act of doing so lightning hit him and killed him. They picked him up, carried him into the cave, and buried him in one of the big rooms. That is the legend of Red Panther. He was the son of the chief." [1]

There are those who are convinced that the story of Red Panther was indeed invented by a writer like Henry Shoemaker, or by the owners of the cave who were trying to attract visitors with a quaint legend. Whatever the case may be, it's interesting to explore any elements of the tale that may have historical precedents. Just fifty years ago, for example, the Amish of Lancaster County would not use lightning rods on houses or barns, preferring instead to have a protective walnut tree growing beside their structures. Their thinking was perhaps similar to, although opposite, that of the Senecas in the Red Panther legend, in that the Amish believed that the walnut tree would somehow attract lightning and divert it from the barn or house. In both cases, however, the beliefs may have evolved from religious tenets. The Amish ideas, for example, could have evolved from early religious warnings by their bishops. In the late 1700's and early 1800's some Scotch-Irish and English ministers, and perhaps clergymen in the various German sects as well, were preaching sermons against the use of lightning rods. Such artificial devices were seen by these pastors as a means to avoid the Almighty's "justifiable wrath" , which, to them, was irreverent defiance of God himself. [2]

Through a similar thought process, the Delaware Indians of Pennsylvania would not use driftwood to build their sweat lodges because they believed this would cause a flood. They also would not build these lodge houses of "thunder-burned wood" (wood struck by lightning) because they were afraid that by doing so they would anger the lightning spirit. This rage, they thought, would then descend upon them in the form of severe storms. [3]

The fact that both the Amish and Delaware Indians alike had convictions related to lightning that were slightly similar to the view related in the Red Panther legend lends an air of authenticity to the old tale, thereby making it even more intriguing to those who like to speculate about such connections. But there is more to the story than just the ideas about lightning and beech trees. There is also the question of how the Indians would have handled the burial of a heathen like Red Panther.

History relates that Indians here in Pennsylvania always treated their dead with utmost respect. The Senecas, for example, would wrap their deceased in skins and place them on scaffoldings. Then they mourned through a ten-day "death feast" [4] It is also recorded that a dead warrior would never be left on the field of battle. His comrades would either come back for him, or drag him away for proper burial. This practice was followed faithfully, as though it were a moral duty.

There may be other pieces of supporting information for the Red Panther legend, and, for that matter, for the Penn's Cave story too. Too much time has passed to know for sure in either case, but Mr. Stover had the last word on the authenticity of Woodward Cave's legend.

"There's another thing I'm going to mention to you. I didn't mention this to anybody, but I did take a family of Seneca Indians through the cave. This has been before the Byrds owned the cave - must've been about twenty-two years ago. This was a family, and they had their mother and grandmother with them. So when we got into the cave there, I gave this history, you know, about the Seneca Indians, and they didn't say much about it. But there was an old lady, she told me she was one hundred and two years old, and I don't doubt her. Her hair was white as snow, and she was an Indian, there was no question about it. She had her hair in braids, and they hung down almost to her knees in the back. And, boy, was she witty.

"So after we showed the cave to them and came back out, this old lady and I sat on the bench over there outside the

7

cave. I got to talking to her. I said, 'What do you think about the history we gave you about the Seneca Indians? Do you believe it?'

"Oh yeah, sure," she said. "That's true. They used to live in caves, inhabited caves."

"I said, 'What about Red Panther?'

"Well, yes. I believe that too, because we do believe that the beech tree is sacred, even up to this day."

"And I said, 'Well, do you think he's buried in there?"

"Well," she said, "I don't know. We didn't bury our dead back in those days. Did you ever read about us putting our dead on scaffolds and letting the Great Spirit take care of them?"

"And I looks at her, and I said, 'Where would he be?'

"She said, 'Well, your cave has a lot of faults, cracks, big cracks, in it. Your dead-end room back there has a beautiful one."

"She walks under it and looks way up. There's one place in there you can see up about sixty five feet.

"And she says, 'There's where they might've buried him - not buried him, but placed him.'

"And I said, 'Well, I'm glad to hear that." [1]

Entrance to Woodward Cave, Centre County
(Winter scene during a snow storm)

WOLF DAYS IN CENTRE COUNTY

John Blair Linn, in his History of Centre and
Clinton Counties, has preserved a story of a wolf encounter that is
probably typical of episodes experienced by early pioneers in many
parts of Pennsylvania. This Centre County incident is said to have
occurred in Bald Eagle Township, probably around 1800:

*In early days wild animals of various kinds were
abundant, and at times very impudent. ... On one occasion, as John
Carskaddon was on his way to a neighbor's, a distance of a mile or two, he
was attacked by a pack of wolves. Their appearance was so sudden, and
they assailed him so furiously, that he barely had time to take his position
against a tree, when he killed several of them with his gun, which he
happened to have with him, before he succeeded in escaping to the house.* [1]

It wouldn't be a pleasant experience for anyone to be
pursued by a pack of wolves, any one of which is probably strong
enough to drag down a man and break his arm or leg with one bite
of its vice-like jaws, and even in cases like John Carskaddon's,
where a person was carrying a musket, being chased by a pack of
wolves would still be a harrowing ordeal. However, there were
times when wolves would pursue someone who was without any
means of defense, and in these cases the experience would have
been nothing less than terrifying. Several such incidents have
been preserved in the oral history of Centre County, and the
following two accounts, both of which have been handed down over

11

the years by the descendents of the individuals that were attacked, reveal unusual strategies that were once employed by unarmed men when they were being chased by a pack of wolves.

The first episode probably occurred in the late 1850's or early 1860's on Big Poe Mountain, near the village of Greenbriar, Penn Township. Around this time, Solomon Lingle, who was born in 1836, lived in a log house west of present-day Poe Dam, where he farmed twenty-five or thirty acres of mountain land. He also "moonlighted", never missing an opportunity to do other jobs which would supplement his meagre income. The story of Solomon Lingle's life and the narrative of his wolf encounter have been saved over time by his descendants, and these accounts preserve a memory of just how tough the people of those times had to be.

"He had a saw mill in Poe Valley, and lived in a sort of lean-to there," recalled Lingle's grandson in 1989. "One day he fell on a saw, and it cut open his stomach. He pushed off with his hands, and they were all cut up. They put him in a tub of water, and his insides were all hanging out. But Doc Frank [probably Dr. George S. Frank who was a physician in Spring Mills and Millheim around 1885] sewed him all up, and he lived a good many years after that.

"He would get fifty cents a day, in those days, for mowing farmers' grass [hay]. Candles were scarce in those days, so at night his wife, Elizabeth, would hold a pitch light for light for him to split shingles. I still have the drawing knife he used to make those shingles.

"They didn't have reapers then to mow. They would cut it with a scythe. He walked all the way out of Poe Valley into Penns Valley with his scythe in the morning and mow grass for the farmers. One day when he come down through the Auman Kettle, in the Zerby Gap up above Greenbriar, he heard a bunch of wolves howling. They wanted to attack him and tried to surround him. He took a stone [the whetstone that was carried by all men who used scythes in those days] and hammered against the scythe, and that chased them away. It scared them." [2]

One other Centre County man had a similar harrowing encounter with a wolf pack, and his story reveals another ingenious way that was used to ward off a band of these grey marauders. The event took place in the wilds of Potter Township, probably in the 1830's or 40's. Once again, the tale has been handed down to the present day by descendants of the man who was attacked by the wolves. Born in 1808, Johnathan Rossman was in his twenties or thirties at the time of the encounter.

"You should probably go back and start with the kind of life Jonathan Rossman had to live," began the family genealogist who had studied the matter. "He lived in a small cabin in Krise Valley, and here he raised seventeen or eighteen children! My grandfather always told me he was one of seventeen, or he was the seventeenth, and I don't recall which it was. Jonathan Rossman lived in there, and he raised that family. He was what we called in those days a laborer. Maybe I could go a little bit further and say he was basically a slave.

"He helped the farmers in Penns Valley; I could name you two families, the Fyes, and the Fishburns. And there were the Mulburgers and the Wagners. He worked for them all summer, and never done anything else. And this is the way he made his living, plus the fact he probably did the same thing by hunting, you know, and stuff like that. Probably he had a little garden or a little patch; this we don't know because of the fact the way things have grown up since I've started worrying about it. But we do know that he probably did a lot of hunting. Probably, if I was to guess, I could say maybe ninety percent of his meat was wild game. He knew a lot about butchering, and he could help people. And in the fall of the year, every day, he would have to walk [from Krise Valley out Boal Gap Road to Colyer in Penns Valley], this was his mode of transportation, to the farmers in our valley and help them butcher.

"You know where he lived and how far he had to travel; he couldn't go the other way because it was too far through the mountains the other way to Colyer. And this is what he probably did every day of his life in the fall. In the olden days you could hunt anytime, as far as that was concerned, but most of the time you were done hunting around Thanksgiving; because this is when, the fall season, you had things to gather together for the winter. And this is what you always had to do. So when it got cold enough in the fall, when it come time for butchering, this is the way he spent his time.

"And, of course, this one particular night as he was going home - probably bloody clothes on, because he wouldn't do like we do today; you know, the butcher has aprons and everything - these wolves started chasing him. How he fended them off we don't know, we only guess. And they found out he was getting where they couldn't attack him anymore or corner him, and as he jumped in the house the wolves jumped on the porch roof. One story has it that the sausage - and this is another story that is hard for you kids and it's hard for us to believe, that a lot of his pay was in produce. There would be some guy would say, 'I'll give you a bushel of potatoes, a half bushel of potatoes.'

"But this particular time, according to the legend and according to the story, and I think it was perfectly right, he had some sausage and butcher meat. And he had fed them all this as he went to keep them from attacking him. This is the way he fended them off so he was able to get to the house. This is the story, and I'm sure by going back and finding out all the stories that we have, this is, without question, what happened. Would you be willing to go out tomorrow, leaving before dark, I mean before daylight, to make, your next appointment? He felt that this was the only way he could maintain his family. This thing come only once't a year, so to speak, to this other guy. If he missed it he was missing some food for his family. So he hesitated not a bit." [3]

There is little reason to doubt that the preceding two Centre County wolf encounters happened much like the oral history says. At least it seems certain that both men were attacked by wolves. However, there may be some legendary elements incorporated into their stories. In other words, parts of older, similar, episodes could have been assimilated into the Lingle and Rossman stories. It is possible, for example, that accounts of similar wolf attacks that actually occurred in seventeenth or eighteenth century Europe were confused with and partially woven into the Centre County folktales. There is, in fact, an Irish folktale that contains events that are intriguingly similar to those recalled in the Lingle and Rossman encounters of Centre County.

The Irish story referred to here has been preserved in a volume of early British history, and it seems worth repeating here, not only because it's such a charming account, but also because it shows that the two tales previously related are, without a doubt, based on fact:

Howell, in one of his "Familiar Letters," written to Sir James Crofts, September 6th, 1624 says: - A pleasant tale I heard Sir Thomas Fairfax relate of a souldier in Ireland, who having got his passport to go for England, as he past through a wood with his knapsack upon his back, being weary, he sate down under a tree wher he open'd his knapsack and fell to some victuals he had; but upon a sudden he was surpriz'd with two or three Woolfs, who, coming towards him, he threw them scraps of bread and cheese till all was done; then the Woolfs making a nearer approach unto him, he knew not what shift to make, but by taking a pair of bagpipes which he had, and as soon as he began to play upon them, the Woolfs ran all away as if they had been scar'd out of their wits. Whereupon the souldier said, "A pox take you all, if I had known you had lov'd musick so well, you should have had it before dinner!" [4]

The similarities between this Irish tale and the Centre County accounts may mean that there was, indeed, some partial transfer of details from the Irish story to the Lingle and Rossman stories. On the other hand, the similarities may just indicate that the methods of using noise or food to fend off attacking wolves was not an uncommon tactic used by those who lived in those thrilling times, not only just in Centre County, but in all parts of Pennsylvania where packs of wolves endangered the lives of people living during a period we now might refer to as Pennsylvania's "wolf days".

THE LOST TREASURE OF PENNS CREEK

Few people today are aware of it, but the tale of *Jack and the Beanstalk* preserves an ancient superstition concerning clouds and the treasures people thought they concealed. It was once accepted that clouds were really the mountains of heaven. Apparently solid and impenetrable, these heavenly peaks occasionally seemed to be split apart by jagged bolts of lightning. During these brief periods, it was believed, mere mortals could get a glimpse of the shining wealth within, "but only for a moment, and then, with a crash, the celestial rocks closed again". [1] Eventually, fantastic tales were told of lucky souls who had wandered into these misty treasure-laden hills and found their fortunes.

It seems that any stories of lost treasure and yarns about those who have sought it are among the most well-liked of all folktales. Everyone enjoys the idea of discovering a vast fortune which he can keep all for himself. People today try to realize such dreams through participation in the many state lotteries which anyone can play for a mere dollar or two, but in the old days peoples' fantasies of getting rich centered around finding buried treasure or stumbling across undiscovered lodes of gold and silver. Then, too, there evolved a set of beliefs centered around where it was most likely you could uncover such wealth and the exact procedures that had to be followed in order to retrieve these concealed riches. So popular and so appealing were these ideas that they were gradually woven into the folklore of the times, thus creating some of the more interesting tales that once could be found in the quaint corners of Penn's Woods.

In the tale of "Jack's Narrows", which appeared in the second volume of this series entitled The Black Ghost of Scotia, and More Pennsylvania Fireside Tales, it was mentioned that people used to believe that great wealth could be found wherever a motionless light would hover over a spot at night. Similarly, it was once held that certain peculiar formations on the ground were indicative of buried riches. Any round bare spots in an otherwise fertile field, or a circular patch of wet ground where the surrounding soil was dry, were believed to be likely places to find buried treasure. More than one person tried to dig into a *Hexedanz*, believing that the fairies had buried their treasure in these odd barren rings. However, it was not just a matter of going out any old time and digging away at will. The hour of the moon had to be just right, and silence had to be maintained throughout the entire time of the excavation. Failure to follow the correct procedures when digging for treasure could result in the loss of the whole thing, as well as possible bodily harm. At least that was what some of the folk wisdom held. Nonetheless, that didn't keep men from trying their luck, and there were certainly enough tales of fabulous caches buried here and there in the mountains to keep any avid treasure hunters working full time.

Almost every county in Pennsylvania has its tale of a fortune in gold or silver that was once lost or hidden and now is waiting to be found by some lucky person. In Sinking Spring Valley of Blair County there is the story of the canoe-load of gold bullion that two men buried in that region. Perry County has its tale of a kettle full of gold that was buried on the site of an Indian burial ground near New Bloomfield. The gold was said to have been given to an Indian squaw by the French in return for English scalps. According to the story, the Indians left the gold behind when attacking white settlers unexpectedly routed them from the area. Potter County has at least two tales of lost gold shipments that have never been found, and in McKean County there is an account of a fortune in silver bars that is buried in the trackless Alleghenies near Smethport. There are many other similar stories, but there is one particular Centre County episode that is typical of many of these types of accounts. It is included here because it also contains many of the supernatural elements that were once woven into such narratives.

According to the folktale that has circulated for at least one-hundred years along Penn's Creek of Penn's Valley, Centre County, there are two saddle bags filled with gold coins that lay buried in the hills beside the creek. The Indians called this beautiful mountain stream *Kayarondinhagh*, but the white man decided the Indian title was not worth keeping, and so, inspired by their own self interests and political agendas, named it "Penn's" Creek. No records seem to have preserved the meaning of the name the Indians assigned to the stream, and, similarly, no one knows today exactly what happened to the gold coins that were once supposedly buried along it, despite the fact that the tale about the coins dates back to a time considerably later than the years when John Penn, son of William Penn, was alive and was honored by having his name placed upon the *Kayarondinhagh* of the Iroquois.

Although the Indians probably had their own ancient legends about the stream now called Penn's Creek, the white mans' legend of the gold coins is set during the days when soldiers-of-fortune, con artists, and land speculators were all moving west to try out their get-rich-quick schemes and to see if their luck would be any better in the "Ohio country" than the cards fate had dealt them to this point in their lives back east.

Among these adventurers, according to legend, were two horsemen who passed through central Pennsylvania carrying their entire fortunes with them. The capital consisted of many gold pieces, which the men had stuffed in their saddle bags. Their intent was to use the money for land speculation, and thoughts of the huge profits they would make probably filled their heads as they traveled through vast forests and unsettled valleys of unsurpassed beauty.

"As they rode along, they became aware that they were being followed," claimed the lady who had heard the legend many years prior to the time she passed it on to me. "So they rode off of the narrow trail that ran through the valley, hid themselves, and buried the gold in a heavily wooded section."

"They decided to separate and each try to reach the upper fort [Potter's Fort]; each man to wait for the other one there. One man did get through, but he had caught a cold, developed lung fever, and died. When the second man had not shown up, and knowing that he was about to die, he told his secret, giving as nearly as possible the location of the buried gold. The story spread, as treasure stories will, and from time to time people have hunted the gold, but no one has ever found it.

"Superstition enters the story, too. The place where the gold was hidden is protected, so it has been claimed. More than fifty years ago, a young man was riding a horse to his home after a late date. When he came to a place in the road, his horse suddenly refused to go any farther. He tried to force him ahead, but the horse jumped to a bank in one swift motion and followed the jump with rearing and trembling.

"At first, the young man could see nothing, but when he looked a little longer, he could see an animal about 12 feet long, from tip of nose to tip of tail, which looked like a panther but had the feet of a deer. It also made a noise; the young man was too scared to do anything but got out of there the fastest way he knew.

22

"He never forgot the spot and neither did the sorrel horse, as it was frightened every time it passed the spot, even in the broad daylight.

"Later as the young man thought it over, he was sure that the animal was trying to show him where the gold was hidden. Many years later, he revisited the place and actually dug at different places which he thought looked like good places to bury gold. He never found the gold, but he never gave up the thought that the gold is there." [2]

According to the lady who passed the preceding account on to me, the man who told her the story and who claimed he had been frightened by the strange animal was her uncle Jerry Corman. The event took place about 1910 near Will Grove's farm on the Beaverdam Road, between Zerby Station and Coburn. Today the small hill where Jerry Corman dug for the gold still stands behind the barn on the Baker farm. Other people also got the idea that there might be gold hidden on the farm, and it is said that former owners of the place once dug a small hill entirely away in efforts to find the treasure. Very few people give much thought to the story today, since it would seem that if there indeed had been a treasure it was probably recovered by the second of the two men who had helped to bury it in the first place and who came back for it at a later date. On the other hand, those who put any faith in the old superstitions about how a buried treasure must be excavated might argue that those who dug in the past just didn't know how to do it the right way. In fact, if the old folktales are to be believed, there were more than several people like that in various Pennsylvania Dutch sections of the state, including that bastion of the race, the Blue Mountains of Berks and Lebanon Counties.

In their fascinating compilation of Pennsylvania German folk stories collected in the Blue Mountains of the Pennsylvania Dutch country in the early decades of the twentieth century, authors Thomas Brendle and William Troxell mention a number of old anecdotes about quests for buried wealth, and these tales also preserve the supernatural aura that once was part of the beliefs about treasure hunting. It seems that even black cats came into play once in a while when people were trying to find a good spot to dig for riches. One suggested method, for example, was to drive a stake in the ground at the spot where the fortune was thought to be buried. Then at night the treasure hunter was to tie a black cat or a black hen to the stake and come back the next morning. "If in the morning the fowl or cat was found torn to pieces, then treasure was there, otherwise not." [3]

The preceding idea begins to touch upon the belief that a buried treasure was oftentimes guarded by something malicious and supernatural. This point was also mentioned in the tale entitled "More Snakes" which appears in *The Black Ghost of Scotia, and More Pennsylvania Fireside Tales* (Volume II of this series). In that tale it is related that snakes were sometimes thought to be guardians of hidden wealth, but there were notions that were even more fantastic than this. One such example is a story from Lebanon County which was said to have occurred shortly after the Revolutionary War.

During this time of upheaval and new beginnings there was a bandit who was the terror of southern Lebanon County, so the story goes. He was very successful in plying his cowardly trade, and since he couldn't exactly take his ill-gotten gains to a bank for safe keeping, the notorious thief elected instead to bury his loot at well-concealed and inaccessible spots in the South Mountain. The work of concealing the plunder would always be done at night so no one would notice, but this made it hard for the criminal to find the places when he wanted to retrieve some of his stash. To overcome the problem the clever thief tied a string to a tree along the mountain pass and stretched it over to the spot where his loot was buried. This marked the hiding place to his satisfaction and enabled him to find it a night, until one day when the string somehow got broken. After that time the treasure was lost, as the thief himself could not find it.

Eventually the robber died, but the stories of his buried cache lingered on, and were convincing enough that a group of local men decided to try their luck at finding it. Before actually starting their search, the treasure hunters agreed to consult a well-known seeress who owned a "magical mirror". Her advice was for the men to go to a particular spot in the area and draw some sort of magical circle on the ground. They were then to dig only within the circle, taking care not to throw any dirt outside of it.

The men drew the circle according to the directions given to them, and then they excitedly began to dig. After a lot of hard labor they dug a hole that was shoulder deep, and then one of the diggers discovered a chest. Just as he was about to cry out that he had found it, he looked up and saw "a large black dog with jaws open and teeth bared ready to leap on him". This sight frightened him so much that he instinctively reacted by striking at the dog with his shovel. A little dirt that was still on the shovel landed outside the circle, and "immediately the dog vanished, and also the chest." [4]

Similar tales of the Blue Mountains told of men finding treasure chests but being thwarted by the sudden appearance of a "ferocious looking boar", or by a dragon, or by the Devil himself. Treasure hunters over in Findland, Montgomery County, for example, once searched for a buried fortune, and had been told that silence had to be maintained "from the time they began to dig until they had the treasure fully in their possession". The men dug away, never saying a word, until they found the chest.

Excited by their good fortune, the men grabbed the handles of the chest and hoisted it above their heads. They had lifted the chest about half way to the surface when one man looked up. He was so surprised and frightened by what he saw that he forgot that silence was to be maintained at any cost, and he yelled "Drop it! The man with the red jacket!' ['Der mit em rode Wammes' - another name used for the Devil]. "Immediately," claims the legend, "the chest disappeared." [5]

This last example from the Blue Mountains shows just how intense the superstition surrounding treasure hunting could be, and, along with the other stories like it, provides clues as to where people might have gotten the idea that frightful beasts once guarded treasures like the one that was said to be buried along Penn's Creek. All kinds of frightful imaginings could occur in the mind of a person who had heard such tales from the time he was young, and who, all of a sudden, was thrown into a set of circumstances that seemed to bring all the old beliefs to life. All it would take would be the night wind wailing through the trees, causing dried leaves and dead branches to rattle like the bones of some forgotten skeleton. Add to this effect some dark clouds flitting across a misty yellow moon which was casting shadows of swaying tree limbs on the road ahead, and the setting would be just right for anyone's imagination to run wild. In this case there was the additional stimulus of the individual passing through the section where a treasure was thought to have been hidden. Perhaps just at that time a large bobcat or mountain lion crossed the road in front of the horseman. That certainly would have been enough to frighten the horse. Moreover, if the cat were big enough, it could have caused the man's mind to work overtime. At that point he might tend to see things that weren't really there at all, such as the subconscious images formed in his mind by tales he had once heard as a boy.

As far as the treasure itself, on the other hand, maybe it's still there. Perhaps another Jack, like the young boy in the fairy tale, will be walking through the woods along Penn's Creek one day and will be distracted by a golden flash of light as the sun is reflected off something partially exposed in a hill along the creek. The boy may decide to investigate and find the long lost treasure at last. If so, he will be hailed as a modern day version of the Jack of fairy tale fame, except he will have had to fight neither giants nor monsters in order to carry away his fortune.

THE TELL-TALE TOMBSTONE

"Innocent until proven guilty" is one of the cornerstones of our legal system, but this seems only to hold true for people who are alive. Sometimes the dead can be unjustly accused, and, with no way to defend themselves, are, in these cases, tried and convicted in the minds of the living without so much as a trial or benefit of a lawyer. Unfortunately there probably have been many situations like this over the years, but there is one in particular that has proved very long-lived, and which, when brought to their attention, can still enrage descendants of the defamed.

This story is not one that is remembered or discussed much anymore, but it does still surface now and then. However, about ninety or a hundred years ago the yarn was well known throughout the many small settlements surrounding the tiny Centre County village of Millheim. The tale probably was at that time a favorite topic of conversation at auctions, flittings, camp meetings, and other social events of the day. Without doubt, the narrative certainly would have been a "hot" item that was often heard around the pot-bellied stoves of country stores in communities like Aaronsburg, Rebersburg, Spring Mills, and Farmers Mills at the turn of the century. There are numerous theories that could be proposed to account for the tale's popularity,

29

but the primary reason that explains why the story was destined to be more than just a "seven day wonder" is that it's the type of account that is designed to activate even the most lack-luster imagination. After all, when you have a murder mystery woven into the plot, and supernatural evidence that seems to lead to the murderer, it's hard for most people not to be intrigued, and to wonder if, indeed, such things can actually happen.

There are at least seven versions of the Millheim legend that have surfaced over the years, but whether the victim of the murderer is a child, another man, or a woman, the instrument of death is always a knife, for if it were something else, then there would be no tell-tale tombstone. However, there does exist just such a graveyard marker, and it sits in a prominent position within the hallowed ground called Union Cemetery - a quaint country burial plot that lies just west of the town whose name, when translated from the German, means "Home of Mills".

The location of the tell-tale tombstone seems appropriate since Millheim is also known for its bleak-looking haunted house which sits on a high knoll on the left side of the road as you enter town from the west. The building was left unoccupied for a long period of time, being mainly used for storage, and signs of neglect became more and more noticeable as the years went by, until finally the place began to take on a look that was more in line with its reputation. However, now (1997) the run-down house is finally being remodeled, or "spruced up" as they might say in that part of the country. Like most old neglected places, this house has, or had, its ghost, but that story will be included in a future volume. It's a tale that is just perfect for a book like this, not unlike that of the tombstone in the Union Cemetery which, although standing almost unnoticed and forgotten these days, preserves the memory of the man who became the target of the vicious rumors that surfaced some years after his death.

It seems that Daniel A. Musser was a success story of no small proportions relative to many of his contemporaries. Born in 1822 into one of the oldest pioneer families of the state, Musser grew up as a farm boy in the Gregg Township area of Centre County, but when he turned eighteen he learned the ways of the miller's trade. The young man had no education beyond that which he had gotten at the country school houses of the day, but he was a fast learner who had inherited some of his father's keen business sense. For two years he successfully managed his father's grist and saw mills, but eventually the pleasant song of the mill wheel lost its charm, and the splashing waters of Elk and Penns Creeks beckoned him on to new adventures and higher accomplishments.

Today a person like Daniel Musser would, no doubt, be called a "Type A" personality; that is, someone who is always active and who seems to be involved in many different things at once. Based on his track record, Musser was not one to let any grass grow under his feet. After leaving the family businesses he went on to establish an impressive list of accomplishments, including being elected deputy sheriff of Centre County and County Treasurer of that same county. He also found the time to be an avid hunter, holder of many township offices, a leader in his church and Sunday-school, a beloved father who raised a family of seven children, and owner of lucrative lumber, tanning, foundry, and flour mill businesses. That he was a very successful man is evident from the fact that at the time of his death in 1888 he owned two large flour mills, as many farms, and other parcels of real estate around Millheim.

Based on such an impressive record of lifetime service and accomplishments, Daniel Musser would seem to be one of those individuals who in his days would have been popularly described as "one of nature's noblemen". However, despite all the evidence to the contrary, Musser was to become known as the perpetrator of a foul crime - a crime which may not have ever even been committed by anyone. Nonetheless, once the story of the deed surfaced it became popular fodder for the gossip mills and slander carriers of the town. To this day the old legend still besmirches the man's name and robs his descendants of the pride that should be rightfully theirs.

Contrary to what one might normally expect, the rumors about Daniel Musser and the crime he was supposed to have committed surfaced only after the man had been dead and buried for about thirty or forty years. What actually started the rumor mills into motion was the appearance of an unusual image on Daniel's impressive tombstone. Shaped from a fine block of granite or some other type rock that would outlast less durable material, Musser's marker stands much taller than those around it. This noticeable difference in height is enough by itself to draw peoples' attention to the memorial, and the fact that it sits close by the main road into town was also, it turns out, another unexpected disadvantage. Musser's family probably thought that such an esteemed member of the community should be buried in a prominent spot in the local cemetery, but they could not foresee that a less visible plot might have been better. How could they have known that nature, in one of her cruel twists of fate, would place a brand on the stone - a mark which would be as insinuative as that of the scarlet "A" which the heroine was forced to wear in Nathaniel Hawthorne's famous novel entitled The Scarlet Letter ?

In Hawthorne's fictional work, Hester Prynne is forced to display a large scarlet letter A prominently on her chest at all times as punishment for having committed adultery. It would be a cruel and unusual punishment, to say the least, having always to display a sign that would let everyone who met you know that you were a sinful outcast, but Daniel Musser's reputation was just as sullied by the mark that was indelibly stamped upon him as well - or, to be more exact, upon his tombstone. For the outline of the knife that mysteriously appeared on the stone, decades after it was put into place, and which some said actually dripped blood at times, was no less damning than Hester Prynne's scarlet letter. The only difference, it might be said, was that Hester was depicted as being alive when she had to bear the abuse of her accusers, whereas Daniel was mercifully spared such shame; instead, it was his ancestors who suffered the injustices of it all.

Perhaps there was a murder, or more than one, in the Millheim area during Daniel Musser's lifetime, and local historians may be able to verify the truth of the matter. However, if there were any crimes like that at all during this time period, it would take a lot of reading through editions of old newspapers to find any details today. No doubt Aaronsburg's *Der Centre Berichter*, published from 1827 through 1871, when it was moved to Millheim and became the *Millheim Journal*, would have published articles on any crime as sensational as murder. Nonetheless, stories recorded on the ephemeral pages of newspapers are not destined to be long-lived, and so a lot of things that were of great importance to the people of that day are no longer even remembered today - even crimes of great passion. Certainly the late Donald Heggenstaller, colorful editor of the *Millheim Journal*, would have been as likely as anyone to know some of the details about past murders in the area, but he knew of none other than the Bill Ettlinger case - an Old West type shoot-out which occurred in Woodward in 1896 and which will be the subject of a story in one of my next volumes.

Heggenstaller, an interested and discerning observer of his fellow country folk, and a dabbler in things unusual and fantastic, had heard several versions of the Musser legend. One of these accounts claimed that a murder supposedly once occurred in the Millheim Hotel, and that Daniel Musser was suspected as the murderer. However, the version that Heggenstaller printed in the *Millheim Journal* was the one that invoked the wrath of several of Musser's descendant's. In 1988, Heggenstaller recalled that story once again, a legend that states that Musser came home one day and found that his new bride had been brutally murdered with a butcher knife. The tale goes on to state that despite his claims of innocence, and evidence supporting that claim, local people still refused to believe the young bridegroom was not the killer, and he was hanged for the crime. In what the tale seems to see as Musser's final desperate attempt to convince his accusers of his innocence, the tormented man is said to have claimed "If I'm innocent you shall know, a knife from my gravestone shall grow." [1]

"Oh my God!", recalled Heggenstaller. "My phone rang from those family members. 'How could I disgrace their name?' Oh, did we have a dandy over that deal! What the tombstone story actually does is, it clears him of this murder that he was supposed to have been blamed for," noted the country editor. "He had made the comment that there'd be a knife. "Well,

I understand by people like old Bob Colyer here in Millheim, who has been dead for twenty-eight years, that it actually happened - that a knife came out of that tombstone and it actually dripped blood. So they turned the tombstone around, and the knife came out on this side again. Then they finally plastered it over, and that didn't do it. Now there's metal plates on both sides. The family says the metal plates were put there because the tombstone cracked and they're trying to keep it together." [2]

Although the tombstone is real, as are the metal plates on it, the idea that Daniel Musser was hanged for his supposed crime is pure fiction, since he died of natural causes. However, the notion that he was responsible for someone else's death seemed to take on a life of its own over the years. One variation of the tombstone legend states that he murdered a child with a butcher knife, and the image of that knife was placed on Musser's gravestone, presumably by supernatural forces of some sort, to identify him as the murderer. Still another rendition of the tale claims he betrayed a young maiden, and then, apparently to keep her from tarnishing his reputation, killed her. It was her vengeful spirit, the last remaining essences of a young mountain maid whose life so full of promise was taken away in such a violent fashion, that caused the knife to appear on the tombstone as evidence of Musser's guilt, or at least that's what this particular version of the legend claims.

There is yet another "spin" on the story, and this one also clings to the theme of the betrayed young maiden. "This here young girl, she might have been fourteen or fifteen, was maybe an orphan or something like that," recalled the popular teller of valley tales. "She had been housekeeping for this Musser family, and the girl became pregnant. Well, she got murdered somehow. They said it was an accident, or, I don't what all, but, anyway, they accused this man Musser of doing it. They never convicted him because, you know people around here, they go by your status. They don't give a damn what you do, as long as you go to church every Sunday and have a lot of money - that's all that matters. So this was his position too. Of course, some of the 'lesser' people accused him; the common people talked. He said if he had killed her there would be a knife on his tombstone." [3]

Injurious as these tales are, it would seem that to some people the smears were not black enough. Although the rumors pointed to Musser as a cold-blooded murderer, there were those who apparently were not satisfied with what the stories claimed was the motive behind the crime. A slaying of a young and helpless woman always made for a good plot in a mystery novel, but there had to be money involved in a real murder story, and Musser obviously wasn't lacking funds; at least that would seem to be a possible explanation for how one other version of the legend surfaced. Whether or not this variant became more popular than the others at one time is impossible to say today, but it certainly had a different "twist" to its plot.

According to this rendition, the murder committed by Daniel Musser happened during the tumultuous war years of 1861 to 1865. The War Between the States certainly was a time, it would seem, that caused everyone's nerves to be a bit more on edge, and so it might occur to someone who wanted to come up with a good story that if a murder were going to be committed it might be during the Civil War.

Despite the anxieties and stresses of that period in Pennsylvania history, the husbandman had to continue his day-to-day tasks, and the business, some in those days would say the back-breaking drudgery, of farming continued as usual. There were still fields to plow, crops to plant, and cattle to raise, and during those times it was a common sight, during the late spring and summer months, to see herds of cattle or packs of horses being driven to market by men called drovers, and it was one such drover that figures in the Civil War version of the Daniel Musser tombstone story.

In order to set the stage for this account from the Civil War years, a few words should first be said about drovers in general. The period from 1810 to 1840 has been described as "the golden age of the drover". [4] Droves of sheep, swine, horses, cattle, and even flocks of turkeys were common sights in certain sections of the state, sometimes more than three or four such groups passing through in a single day. Apparently there were enough economic incentives to warrant such drives, among which was the fact that local farmers would, it seems, buy some of this moving stock along the way as the drover guided his animals through mountains and valleys of the back country - sections where roads were almost impassable to wagon traffic during the spring thaws, but which could still be traversed by four-legged travelers no matter how deep the mud. It was a possibility, then, that either going to or coming back from market, the drover might be carrying cash. This was a fact that didn't escape the inventor of the Musser legend that is set during the Civil War.

After a hundred years there is not much left except the "bare bones" of the story, but the report was probably always sketchy. After all, it's pretty hard to come up with details sometimes when there is no honest basis for the tale in the first place. Nonetheless, the legend from the 1860's states that in those days drovers would bring horses and cows through Penns Valley, "selling them as they went". The drovers, as was noted earlier, carried the money they made with them, and one morning one of these itinerant cowboys was found in a ramshackle barn just outside Millheim. The man had been murdered with a knife, and he had been robbed. It was from this ill-gotten gain, the tale claims, that Daniel Musser got his start, for it was Musser, continues the legend, who murdered the unfortunate drover. [5]

This account of the murdered drover was probably as earnestly told and as fervently believed as all the other versions of the legend. However, at some time or another each variation of the tale was no doubt touted as the one true story behind the damning evidence, evidence in the form of a strange image, that actually did appear on Daniel Musser's tombstone. There is no doubt that a stain or flaw, roughly in the shape of a knife, did eventually become visible on the Musser grave marker. Many people saw the likeness, and most agreed that it certainly looked like a knife blade. What was even more wondrous, however, was the place where this instrument of death appeared: on a sacred place like a tombstone. There had to be something supernatural about the whole thing, and through the 1920's spectators were still lining up to get a look at the marvelous picture. The more people looked at it, the more bizarre it seemed, and soon stories surfaced that claimed the dagger would actually drip blood at certain times, particularly when it rained.

Local children, especially those living near the cemetery, were often scared to go out at night, but Daniel Musser's descendants were mortified by the tales, and they finally took steps to eliminate the ugly scar on the stone. Local tales say the family tried a number of different approaches, including using acid to dissolve the image, turning the stone around, replacing the whole marker at least twice, and so on. But in all cases the image came back. Finally a metal plate was placed over the accusing mark, and that seems to have done the trick, although there are those that say that on rainy days a strange substance oozes out from under the metal plate - a substance that looks like blood.

To those who look for logical explanations to such things, and this writer is among them, let it be said that flaws do occasionally appear in rocks, and they often do bear a close resemblance to a real object. Moreover, when this happens on a tombstone, and it sometimes does, all sorts of weird, and oftentimes malicious, tales surface about the person the stone memorializes. In fact, there are at least two such instances that should be mentioned, either one of which should provide comfort to the long-suffering descendants of Daniel Musser.

The first prominent case of a tell-tale tombstone involves a marker in the cemetery at Bucksport, Maine. Here a memorial to Colonel Jonathan Buck has fascinated the curious for almost a hundred and fifty years. Jonathan Buck was the founder of the town that still bears his name, and, like many of his contemporaries, the colonel was a strict believer in the old Puritanical beliefs, including the idea that a witch should not be allowed to live. One unfortunate elderly woman in the colonel's settlement was accused of being a witch, so the story goes, and the autocratic town father ordered her to be burned. The woman expired in the flames, which burned off one of her legs, but before she died she was able to curse the colonel, screaming that upon his tombstone would appear a sign that would mark him as the

41

murderer of an innocent woman. Johnathan Buck died in 1795, and for fifty-seven years his marker of gray Maine granite stood unblemished. Then, in 1852, people began to notice an unusual outline on the stone, a form that looked like the leg and foot of a woman.

Although the Johnathan Buck legend begins to show that there are, indeed, other tombstone flaws that have lead to fantastic stories, the Maine image is not that of a knife. However, the second prominent legend involving a tell-tale tombstone is one that falls closer to home, and this story does involve many facets that closely resemble the Millheim legend, including the picture of the knife on the grave- stone.

This other Pennsylvania tell-tale tombstone sits in a small country graveyard in Sullivan County. It is not altogether unfitting that this would be the place where the marker sits, since such morbid curiosities need to be surrounded by something uplifting and beautiful - a place like Sullivan County. Justly called Pennsylvania's "Highlands", Sullivan County is home to wonderful natural wonders like the majestic World's End State Park and beautiful Eagles Mere Lake, but it also has its share of legends, including the one about the Sullivan County man who was condemned to die in the electric chair for killing another man with a knife.

The Sullivan County murderer claimed he was innocent, and loudly proclaimed that he hoped the Almighty would mark his tombstone somehow to show the truth. After the man had been executed, his family erected a nice tombstone over his resting place. The dead man's wish about a mark on his gravestone did not take long to materialize, for shortly after the marker was erected an outline that looked like a knife began to materialize on the surface of the granite. Then as time wore on, the image took on more definite detail and people could clearly see something under the dagger: spots that looked like drops of blood dripping off the blade.

Immediately people concluded that God put the tell-tale image on the stone to show that the dead man had not been unjustly put to death; he was a murderer after all. Such talk disturbed the man's family, and so they chiseled the image off the marker. However, the image came right back in short order, and so the relatives decided to replace the stone with another. That did not keep the unholy stain from coming back, and "the same thing happened again - the dagger and the blood." [6]

Since it can now be seen that several "bloody" accounts like that of the Musser tombstone legend have surfaced in other areas over the years, it is left to readers to decide whether or not the legend of Millheim's tell-tale tombstone preserves underlying evidence that points to Daniel Musser as a murderer. However, the fact that strikingly similar tales and circumstances have appeared in other places is reason enough to have little faith in any historical truths claimed by the legend. Moreover, given the history of the man, and noting his many positive accomplishments, it seems more than safe to say that he has been wrongfully accused these many decades. Perhaps there was a murderer who committed a crime as dastardly as one of those detailed in a version of the Millheim legend, but it's unlikely that the culprit was the man who a biographer of the times once described as one whose "home and family stood first in his affections, and throughout his wedded life the dearest place on earth was his own fireside." [7]

The Tell-tale Tombstone in Union Cemetery
Millheim, Centre County

45

TAKING FIRE FROM A GUN

As years went by and I collected more and more legends and folktales from many different parts of Pennsylvania, I began to see that quite a few of the same stories that had circulated during the 1800's were still alive and well during the 1900's. Stories of fantastic animals, fabulous treasures, lonely ghosts, and mysterious witches had not disappeared altogether, but they were fading fast. In fact, today you would not be able to hear many of the types of tales that I could still find just twenty-five years ago, and this is especially true of the witch tales. Among the strangest types of stories a collector could find in those days, the old-time witch stories provide us with some entertaining reading and a reminder of something we all should take seriously right now.

I would expect that many readers of these old-style witch tales will sooner or later begin to think that the people who lived on the farms, in the wooded valleys, and on the rugged mountain slopes of rural Pennsylvania at the turn of the century had a special feeling about their time and place: a feeling that there was, indeed, something marvelous and mystical about these grand hills after all. Some of these feelings were certainly due to the superstitions that were entrenched in the culture of the mountains, but there was more to it than that. The rest of the basis for this attitude can easily be found today, just by looking out over the vistas offered from some of our mountain peaks, or by taking a hike through the grandest parts of our forests. However, we need to remember that this is a vulnerable environment and then take the steps necessary to preserve it for all time. If we don't, it will disappear, leaving future generations with the feeling that we didn't understand the mechanisms of nature any better than those who once believed in witches.

One of the things that surprised me the most in talking to old-timers about their witch tales was the idea that at one time people believed in supernatural explanations for natural phenomena that most of us fully understand today. I heard some very strange stories over the years, a few of which have appeared in the first two volumes of this series, and among the strangest were the tales about game that could not be shot due to the fact that a witch had placed a spell upon it or upon a hunter's gun. This was once a very common type of story that could be heard wherever Pennsylvania hunters gathered to talk of the chase, and they even had explanations as to how it was all done. In fact, one of their ideas was that a witch could, in the Pennsylvania Dutchman's language, *es feier nemme,* or "take the fire from the gun." [1] At one time in Pennsylvania Dutchland there were many who believed that such a thing was possible: that a witch or powwower could invoke a charm that would render someone's gun harmless. It was thought that this effect was accomplished either by preventing the powder from igniting or by causing the shot to dribble harmlessly out the end of the gun barrel after the powder discharged.

Beliefs like this were more prevalent in the days when a man's rifle was a muzzle-loader - the kind that Davy Crockett or Daniel Boone once carried. Notoriously slow-loading, the so-called "Kentucky" rifle was made by Swiss and German gunsmiths in Pennsylvania for use on the frontier in the 1700's. These rifles improved as decades went by, but they could still misfire if the priming hole was clogged or if the powder was damp. In fact, the expression "flash in the pan" comes from the flintlock rifle days when a man pulled the trigger to fire his gun and the only thing that happened was the flash and the smoke of the powder in the rifle's firing "pan", which was the flat outer surface directly above the priming hole. [2] Just enough gun powder was placed on the pan to ignite the powder in the hole, which, in turn, ignited the powder in the rifle barrel. It took a steady aim to hit anything with a flintlock, due to the delay between the time the trigger was pulled and the instant the gun actually discharged. Needless to say, if a man pulled the trigger and made a concentrated effort to remain absolutely steady until the gun discharged, he would be a little upset if nothing happened. However, his patience would be even more severely tried if his gun's misfiring meant a particularly nice buck would fall to another hunter's bullet, or that he didn't get that grouse or rabbit for his family's next meal.

Unshootable grouse seem to be a favorite game animal when it comes to tales of witches "taking fire" from guns, and such stories have been around a long time. Berks County had its share of such yarns, and undoubtedly most other Pennsylvania Dutch sections of Pennsylvania did as well. Probably one of the most well-known of these types of anecdotes in central Centre County involves one of that county's best-known powwowers, Bennie Ripka of Spring Mills.

Ripka was famous over a wide area for the miracles he could perform in counter-acting the spells of bad witches. He was often called upon to cure sick cattle, to quiet crying children, or to help anyone in general who thought they had been bewitched in one way or another. There were many stories about the sly conjurer's feats that made the rounds over the years, and one of these concerned the time that he was accused of taking fire from a gun.

Ben Ripka was never known for his hunting exploits, but he did have a collection of old muzzle-loading rifles at his homestead in the gap that was named after his family. Here in Ripka Gap, an isolated cut through the wilds of Big Poe and Sand Mountains, Benjamin Ripka tended an apple orchard on land that had belonged to his family since the early 1800's. Ripka farmed some of the land, but in back of his house, on soil which was not suitable for farming, he grew apple trees. His stand of trees produced plenty of fruit annually, enough that he could make cider to sell to others. That he was somewhat successful in his efforts is evidenced by the fact that he eventually made wooden barrels in which to sell his apple "squeezings". Perhaps he even had a large steam-driven cider press, like those so popular at that time, to dice and squeeze the apples fed into it. If so, it may have been one much like Harry Neff's old press that has been preserved and is still used every fall at the mountain estate known as The *Bergheim* in Decker Valley of Centre County (For those who are intrigued by unusual names and their origins, I should mention here that Cider Press Road, near the village of Potters Mills, was named after Neff's press, which once stood along this country byway).

However, what does seem certain after all this time is that for many years when the invigorating spell of autumn spilled over the land, turning leaves to gold, tinting skies with the purest of blues, and cloaking awakening valleys with a blanket of morning white, Ben Ripka could be found cider pressing or making cider barrels. His hard work kept him fit, or so it would seem, since he's remembered as being a "fairly tall and thin" man, and "never too dressed up". [3] Jared Ripka, an old-time lumberman from Spring Mills, also recalled that his powwowing relative was a bit of a prankster; or as Jared put it, Bennie "liked to put something over on others". [3] This bit of interesting detail seemed to remind Jared of one particular incident where Bennie's sense of humor led to some hard feelings: the time when "old man" Billy

Walburn thought he was going to have a nice roasted grouse for supper, but got mad instead.

It seems that Billy Walburn showed up at Ben Ripka's cider barrel shop one day after noticing three grouse perched in a couple of Bennie's apple trees out back. He asked Bennie if he could borrow one of his muzzle-loaders to shoot the birds. After "studying" the situation a while, Ripka took down one of his flintlocks and handed it to Walburn, commenting, "Here, take this one; it's loaded too". Walburn immediately went out back, took aim, and fired at the birds in the apple trees. At first it must have seemed to the rifleman that the birds were deaf, because, even though he had gotten fairly close, when the gun went off the birds didn't even fly away. Then probably as he thought about this more and more, and finally was unable to convince himself there was a natural explanation for the bird's seeming indifference to his attack, Walburn began to think of other explanations, settling upon the idea that Ripka had "taken the fire" from the gun.

The cider maker categorically denied the charge, and handed his accuser another muzzle-loader, saying "Here, take this one". This was too much of an insult for the old man, and he "stormed off in a huff !" Just as Walburn was stomping away, Bennie took the second gun, went out back and shot two grouse with one shot. After picking the dead birds up, Ripka stated that he would "just take these over and give 'em to Walburns."

However, that was to be a harder task than it would seem, for when the grouse were offered to the Walburns, the old man refused them, even though his family was poor. He was still "fallen out" with the man who took the fire from his gun. [3]

There are other similar accounts like this that could once be heard in these mountains, and it seems each one has its own unique flavor. Take this next example, where a woman was suspected of taking the fire from several hunters' guns. The setting for this tale is in an area of Centre County called The Loop, noted for the confusing way the many country roads through here wind around in a manner that can bewilder the unsuspecting traveler.

"When they went up through [The Loop] with their shotguns," recalled the son of the man who was one of the frustrated hunters mentioned in the story, "some old woman said 'Where're you goin'? And they said, 'For grouse!' She said, 'Aw, you ain't gonna get anything today anyway!' They went up there, and they shot and they shot, and they shot. Nothing! They saw lots of them, and they couldn't hit them!.

"When they come back down through, the old woman met them at the yard gate. She was holding her apron up, and she says 'Here boys, I'll give you your shot back.' And Daddy said her apron was full of it. He said, 'I seen that with my own eyes!' [4]

Although witches' spells were once believed to have saved quite a few grouse from the deadly fire of a hunter's gun, rabbits too were thought to be sometimes protected in the same way.

"The mountains was full of witchcraft," claimed the life-long country girl who was born in 1904. "In Poe Valley, the Confers, the Aumans, and the Oxenreiders lived in there. Yeah, them Confers and Aumans were noted for that."

"I was in there, right there at Voneida Gap where you go up through to the left," continued her husband. "There was a lot of weeds in there, and, thinks I, I'll just drive over there and I'll shoot a couple rabbits. I took the twelve gauge [shotgun] and went over there. There was lots of rabbits, but I couldn't hit 'em. I shot the weeds away, and I couldn't get 'em. They just hopped away!

"Well, I blamed Ralph L. and his wife. They live right below. I blamed them. They seen me go up, and they heard me shoot. They were in that kind of business. You know, after that I couldn't hit nothin' with that gun!" [5]

One other long-time resident of the same area had a similar problem one day when he was out hunting for rabbits. School teacher Clarence Musser was not a superstitious person, and so was not easily swayed by talk of enchanted game or of witches who would take the fire from a man's gun. Although he was born in 1884 when superstition still ruled a lot of peoples' lives, Musser had acquired enough education to know a little bit about the natural laws of the universe. He knew that the old wives' tales about witches and their seemingly supernatural powers were just poor attempts to explain away events that, in all probability, had logical explanations if enough thought and time were devoted to an investigation.

Armed with this kind of rational thinking, Musser did not hesitate a minute one day in 1907 when he decided to hunt rabbits up on the Brown farm near the quaint burial ground known as the "mountain cemetery". The would-be rabbit hunter knew that a man named "Hen" Zerby, who had a reputation as a powerful witch, lived in this area, and that Zerby's greatest fame came from his power to bewitch animals so no hunters could shoot them. In fact, general opinion was that the mountain wizard had the whole area around him enchanted so that no one who hunted here could shoot a deer, a grouse, a rabbit, or any other kind of game.

"I said I'd get rabbits," recalled the old school teacher in 1971. "I was teaching at the 'mountain schoolhouse' in those days, and I lived there during the week, only going home to Madisonburg on weekends. I borrowed John Lingle's shotgun one fall day during rabbit season, and I went in to Hen Zerby's; his place was the next one after the Piney Camp hunting lodge. He had a little black hunting dog which had a good reputation as a rabbit hound, and I asked him if I could borrow it. He said, 'You can borrow it, but you von't get any ting'!

"I took the dog and went up onto the Brown property, which is west of the mountain cemetery. Many times I found Craters' cows roaming here and returned them. Well, the dog kicked out a rabbit, but I shot at another one I thought I saw in some mountain laurel along the road by a swamp. I went in and looked for the one I thought I had shot and couldn't find a trace of him, dead or alive. I hunted some after that, but I didn't see any more rabbits, or any other game, that afternoon, and when I returned the dog to Zerby, he just laughed." [6]

Clarence Musser attributed the strange events of his ill-fated rabbit hunt to imagination. However, he also said it was almost dark by the time he got back to the mountain schoolhouse. I often thought of him winding his way back down the mountains that fall evening after the odd episode with the rabbits, and I can't help but wonder if his pace picked up as he noticed darkness creeping in around him.

In the Blue Mountains of Berks and Lehigh Counties there was once a story about a hunter like Clarence Musser, but this Nimrod went into the woods to hunt squirrels. He saw quite a few of the animals, and shot and shot, but "was unable to bring any down". Then the man detected a particularly large squirrel and fired at it. However, he missed this one as well, but just then he noticed "a little old grey man hiding behind the bole of a nearby tree." The hunter took a dime, which was silver in those days, not the copper-clad variety we have today, and loaded it into his gun, noting "I'll show that thunder-weather a thing or two". He then fired the gun into the tree top, whereupon "the little old man disappeared". Since silver bullets were thought to be the most effective way to kill a witch or bewitched animals, the story concludes by noting that "from then on the hunter shot without missing". [7]

Belief in stories like the preceding ones and about bewitched game in general was, no doubt, reinforced when people saw the formula for doing the bewitching in black and white. John George Hohman, that widely-accepted authority on such matters in those days, spelled out exactly how to prevent anyone from killing game, and it was easily accomplished just by saying:

(Name of person), shoot whatever you please; shoot but hair and feathers with and what you give to poor people. In the name of The Father, The Son, and The Holy Ghost. [8]

Perhaps people living around Hen Zerby, or near others with similar reputations, also recalled the stories of "little grey men of the woods" when hunters spoke of the local game being hard to shoot or to find. Many folks probably found such tales to be a satisfactory explanation for the hunters' results, but they might have done better if they had looked for other explanations as well. For instance, in Hen Zerby's case, there may have indeed been a shortage of game in the area surrounding Zerby's place.

Remembered by some of his neighbors as "the nicest person you could ever live around", Zerby was also known as an avid hunter. [9] It's recalled, for example, that one fall day while helping some neighbors butcher, Zerby and his son Jim heard some turkeys calling on the top of a nearby ridge. Zerby immediately declared his services at an end, stating that he wanted to track the birds down. With that, he and his son "dropped everything" and went off hunting. [5] Dedicated hunters like that could easily reduce the number of turkeys and other game animals in an area over a period of time, and, in fact, it was recalled that Hen Zerby shot thirteen turkeys during one year in particular. Individual harvests like this were perfectly legal in those times - in the days before game laws were enacted, strictly enforced, and accepted as something necessary for prudent wildlife management. Consequently, when looking back, it seems fair to say that although they were not exactly like the legendarily acclaimed "little grey men of the woods", mountaineers like Henry Zerby did manage, in their own way, to achieve somewhat the same results.

HAIRY JOHN

Near the eastern edge of Centre County, where its boundary line with Union County is defined, there is a natural gap, or "cut", through the mountains that connects the villages of Woodward, Centre County, and Hartleton, Union County. This gloomy defile, popularly known as Woodward Narrows, is always filled with deep shadows in some spots, and even at midday on some days the forest here is home only to whispering pines, restless oaks, and the soft murmur of Voneida Run as it courses through the cool mists of the dark forest. Due to lack of human habitation and to infrequent traffic, the mountain pass often seems like one of those places where few people care to tarry and where time itself appears to have stopped. However, despite its somber and melancholy atmosphere, this quaint little corner of woodland is surrounded by acres of state forest, and so it holds many attractions for the nature lover.

Like other state forest preserves, the mountain acres around Woodward Narrows provide an ideal habitat for wild turkeys and deer, a fact that hasn't escaped the many hunters that are drawn here every hunting season. It's a scenic territory, typical of many of the beautiful woodlands preserved as state forest land here in Pennsylvania, and so it also appeals to hikers, campers, and picnickers who take advantage of the refreshing forest breezes, nature's air conditioning, during the hot summer months. However, there is also one other attraction here that has probably drawn the merely curious to the site for decades.

Along the northern side of Route 45, the state highway that passes through the Woodward Narrows, there is an interesting sign-board which advertises "Hairy John's" forest preserve. The strange name is almost guaranteed to cause even the most passionless individuals to take a second look as they pass by, but it especially appeals to those who wonder about such things. In this case a little curiosity is justified, for the story of "Hairy John" is an interesting one. It's an account that has never been formally recorded in any official biography, and it's not a tale that's remembered much at all today. However, the details of exactly who he was and why he was accorded the honor of having a state forest preserve named after him are all parts of local legends that still cling to this mini-wilderness formed by the towering heights of Winkelblech, Sand, and Thick Mountains.

The site of "Hairy John's" Park is located in the Bald Eagle State Forest of Centre and Union Counties, a picturesque region which was the home of many romantic and thrilling episodes of the long ago. Narratives of panthers, wolves, Indians, ghosts, and witches were once quite plentiful here, but the story of Hairy John was probably one of the favorites. It was, no doubt, often repeated around the cracker barrels of local country stores and beside the hearths of remote mountain cabins. Beside cozy inglenooks on cold winter evenings children heard the tale from their parents and grandparents, passing it on to their own children over the years, and so it has come down to us today. However, it was not really that long ago that John Voneida could be found in his little cabin in the narrows that would later bear his name. In fact, not too many decades ago there were people still alive who remembered seeing the old hermit come into Woodward to buy molasses and other necessities, or to visit his brother Henry who lived at the foot of the *Rundkupf*, or Roundtop, Mountain.

Roundtop Mountain towers over the town of Woodward like a dark and silent sentinel, and can be seen from miles away when approaching the hamlet. However, it is not for old Roundtop that Woodward was once noted. In fact, the thing that really set Woodward apart from the other settlements around it at one time was the pleasant smell of wood smoke that came from the town's many wood burning stoves. Anyone entering the village around mealtime, even just forty years ago, would immediately notice the pungent odor coming from the clouds of smoke that were reminders of an earlier time - a time when butcherings, apple butter boilings, corn huskings, and quaint mountain characters like Hairy John were part of the everyday rural life here.

Although hardy mountaineer types of all kinds had passed through Woodward since 1818, when stage coaches traveling between Bellefonte and Northumberland stopped at Henry Roush's tavern in the Woodward Narrows, none of these folks seems to have made a lasting impression on anyone. However, the hermit of the Narrows is still remembered today, including the fact that his quiet entrances into the sleepy village of Woodward always marked the signal for the children of the town to run and hide from the hairy little man. Voneida's long hair and lengthy beard must have been intimidating to youngsters, but it was probably the tales they had heard their folks tell about him that really made them afraid.

John Voneida's past was clouded by a terrible story, and many people probably feared him because of it. Nasty rumors surrounded the kindly recluse - rumors that insinuated he couldn't get along with his wife, and finally left her to live a solitary existence in the mountains. Harsher stories claimed that "he mistreated his wife, and then ran into the woods to live away from her," [1] or even that "he was accused of killing his wife". [2] But the diminutive recluse denied any such gossip, preferring instead to show people he was a harmless and good-hearted person. One of the ways he polished his image was by offering food and drink to travelers passing by his remote cabin located in the lonely mountain pass near Woodward. There are others who say that he even acted as a sort of wayside postmaster, allowing travelers to leave messages for other travelers at his forest home. Nevertheless, despite Voneida's best attempts, the rumors about him persisted, mainly because they were based on true events.

Older folks who once knew the man related that he had lived in Nittany Valley, probably at Jacksonville, before settling near Woodward. These same oral traditions go on to state that when he lived in Jacksonville he was married to a young lass of the mountains named Susanna, daughter of George Hoy of Madisonburg. The old legends don't say much more about her, except that she was mentally unstable, or "feeble-minded", in the terminology of those days. One day her tortured mind could find no peace and she hanged herself in the closet of their home. Rumors must have run amok, for people in those times had little understanding of mental illness, and so tongues wagged that Voneida's wife hadn't committed suicide, but that Voneida had actually hanged her himself. Children heard their parents' accusations and cruelly taunted the bereaved widower whenever they saw him in the streets. This was more than Voneida could stand, and eventually he was driven away, preferring a solitary life in the mountains to neighbors of any kind. Here he took on the look of a typical recluse, letting his hair and his beard grow long, until people gave him his nickname, "hairy" John. [3]

John Voneida was apparently of a studious turn of mind because, according to the legends, he spent part of his time in the Woodward Narrows by writing a "philosophy" of some sort. In fact, the last fourteen years of his life were said to have been spent in this pursuit. No one today seems to know much about the treatise that Voneida is supposed to have penned, if he actually did write one. Perhaps, with diligent searching, copies can be found in some of the larger libraries in the state, but they are probably very rare.

The little hermit's *taufschein*, or birth certificate, a beautiful piece of fraktur colorfully decorated with tulips, hearts, distelfinks, and other typical "Pennsylvania Dutch" motifs, has been preserved by Voneida descendants, and can still be seen today. The date of birth on the certificate is almost indecipherable, but is most likely November 27, 1815 or 1837. The certificate is entirely written in German script, with the names of the parents given as Johannes Von Neida and wife Susannah. Although his birth certificate still exists, John Voneida's grave site may be harder to find. He is said to be buried in a cemetery near Madisonburg, Centre County, but the inscription on the tombstone may now be so well-weathered that it is almost indecipherable too. Since historical facts are so sparse, the only other way we may hope to find any details about this strange character is to turn to the cloudy and unreliable stories of oral tradition.

These traditional tales recall that John Voneida was a determined deer hunter, exhibiting unusual persistence in "bagging" his quarry. "One of the things I heard," recalled one present-day hunter, "and I don't know if it's true or not, but when he'd hunt deer and see the tracks, he'd just keep on 'em until he'd finally get it - day and night." [4] A contemporary of Voneida's, who was also known for his determination when it came to tracking deer, was Joshua Roush of Woodward. More will be said about this hardy devotee of the chase in a future volume, but for now it can be noted that Roush was famous for his technique of catching live deer. It was this technique, however, that resulted in a little-known episode of the Woodward Narrows concerning how Roush and his deer disrupted John Voneida's quiet life-style one night.

Tales of Joush Roush's stamina and single-mindedness during the chase are still kept alive by his descendants, and one such memory recalls that "he had a pack of dogs that could, and did, trail a deer until it was so tired that the dogs could corner it and hold it until Joush could get it." [5] Live deer could be sold to zoos or game parks, and Josh Roush's pack of dogs were trained to help capture outstanding specimens. Just as a pack of determined wolves keeps chasing a deer until it can't run anymore, Roush's dogs hounded a stag until it dropped. Once the deer was in this state, Roush could easily rope it and carry it back to his deer pens, which stood beside his home on the mountain back of Woodward. It was a capture like this one day, so say the legends, that resulted in a lively evening for Hairy John Voneida.

Josh and his dogs would track a deer for miles, over rugged mountain peaks, down into dark and mysterious ravines, and through tangled laurel thickets. Day and night the chase would continue, until either the deer was captured or it managed to throw the dogs off its scent by walking up a swift creek. Late one day, after following a particularly large buck for many miles,

Roush and his dogs cornered the stag on Winkelblech Mountain, just above Woodward. Here the rugged Nimrod rushed up to the winded deer and threw it down, "bull-dogging" it like a rodeo cowboy. After tying the deer's legs together, Roush flung it over his shoulder and started for home.

The sun was sinking lower and lower in the sky, and soon its last rays were barely visible over the solemn outlines of Shriner Mountain to the west. In a few minutes it was dark, and the tired hunter decided he would stop at John Voneida's cabin for the night. It was a safe haven from the panthers and wolves that roamed the mountains, and Roush knew he would be welcomed by the hermit. Even though wolves and mountain lions were becoming scarce, there were undoubtedly still enough of them around to force a person to be cautious.

Just as Roush expected, John Voneida welcomed his wayward guest and told him that he, and his hog-tied deer, could spend the night safely inside the hermit's cabin. The two men laid the deer in one corner of the place, and, after checking that the animal's feet were securely tied, crawled into their beds and drifted off to sleep. Sometime in the middle of the night the stag managed to get loose. Half crazy with fright, the confused animal began running around the room. The building's other two occupants were rudely awakened, probably by the sound of clattering pots and pans as they were knocked from shelves and tables by the frenzied deer. Somehow the sleepy men managed to recapture the stag and tie it up again, this time taking extra care that the beast could not escape. "Whether the men were able to get any more sleep is anyone's guess!" [5]

The adventure of the rampaging deer was not an episode that would have been appreciated by the fairer sex, and so the incident probably occurred before the time that another woman entered John Voneida's life. Eventually John's grief over his wife diminished to a point where he longed for female companionship once more. The local folk tales say that he did finally find a suitable companion to share his lonely lifestyle, but they have very little else to say about this obscure person. It seems that not much was ever known about the woman. Some say her name was Twila Montray, but this is not certain since her origins seem lost. She may have been what was then known as a "half-breed", the derogatory term used in those days for the offspring of a union between an Indian squaw and a white man. In any case, it would appear that John and his female companion found some happiness for a while. However, Voneida's life was destined to be plagued by tragedies. Tragic events prompted him to begin his peaceful existence in the Woodward Narrows, and it was the same kind of violent actions that ended that existence.

Perhaps the little hermit made some enemies because of the way he lived or because of the way he always frightened the children of the area. On the other hand, maybe a few robbers felt that there was a horde of cash hidden in the hermit's cabin. In any case, Voneida apparently became a marked man in the eyes of a few jaded individuals. He must have seemed an easy prey to ruffians, since he is remembered as being a small, thin, man, and it seems certain that it was several such cowards who set upon the harmless little hermit one day and beat him so badly that he fled the area. The old stories say that Voneida lingered for a while after the beating, but finally succumbed to the severe injuries he had sustained. Apparently he retreated to Madisonburg to try to recuperate, for this is where he is supposed to be buried.

Twila Montray's fate is not as clear, although some say she also was beaten to death by the same ruffians that attacked Hairy John. If that is true, then it is no wonder that John Voneida could not recover from his beating. His heart and spirit were probably broken as well.

Legends are kinder than history when it comes to describing the fate of Hairy John and his Twila Montray. Folktales indicate that John had always expressed the wish that he could become a beech tree when he died and that this is what happened. These same narratives don't say where any such tree may be found in the park, but a few people do claim that a commemorative tree of some type was planted on the site of the little hermit's cabin. Details about Twila Montray's fate are as obscure as the specifics about her life, but some say "there is a story that her spirit haunts the Narrows." [6] Indeed, such tales would appear to have us believe that Twila Montray's ghost flits through the Woodward Narrows, particularly on peaceful summer nights when winds are low, the moon is full, and whippoorwills call from the depths of laurel thickets on Winkelblech Mountain.

Although it would seem a cruel fate for Twila Montray to be destined to haunt the Woodward Narrows for eternity, there may be a kinder interpretation to the ending of this tragic tale. Apparently the idea behind the story of Twila's ghost is that she is lingering in the Woodward Narrows to be near the beech tree that holds the spirit of John Voneida. The notion that victims of violent deaths come back to haunt the scenes of their demise is a typical folktale motif found throughout the world. In the case of Hairy John and his sweetheart it would appear that legend has picked up where life, in its harshness, wrote an unsatisfactory ending. Those of a more romantic bias preferred to believe that John Voneida would have his sweetheart near him for all time; their two spirits inseparably bound forever.

Epilogue:

One fall evening about twenty-five years ago, a young couple was driving through the Woodward Narrows and had an experience that some might say substantiates the Twila Montray ghost story in a convincing way. It was about 9:30 in the evening, and the night is remembered as being clear and beautiful, with no fog to diffuse the car's headlights. The vehicle was heading west, towards the little village of Woodward and had passed Hairy John's Park about two miles back. Suddenly, out of nowhere, something appeared in front of the automobile.

"It looked more like fog, but it was definitely moving," explained the man who was driving at the time. "It wasn't a bright patch, but it was something, and it was in motion. As soon as we got up there it was in motion, left to right, almost as if it was going across the road. And during the time we passed through it, it was almost as if we stood still for a second!"

"We went right through it, and it wasn't fog," continued the man's wife. "We really thought we were hitting something. It was big, I mean it was bigger than a deer. It was an image like of a person. I couldn't make out any shape like a head, a person, or a deer, or anything like that, but there was a mass of something! I grabbed the dashboard and screamed, and he hit the brakes and was stopping."

"I thought I hit a deer, but there was no obvious bump, or anything like that," interjected the husband. "I felt like there was definitely something there and that there should've been a thump or a bump, or like we hit something! It was just kind of like a swoosh! It almost seemed as if she stalled or something, but I stopped the car, and I said, 'What the hell was that?' It was almost as if I should've hit something. I said, 'Let me get out and look.' I checked the car; there was nothing. I walked back around and looked there, and on the road, and there was nothing. When I was walking back there, I really felt creepy. I mean it was obvious there is something wrong here, and I don't know what it is! I got back in and I said 'That was really weird!' It was almost if maybe we drove through a ghost or something like that!" [7]

The sign at Hairy John's Park
and view of the Woodward Narrows .

TOOTH AND CLAW

In his interesting history of northwestern Pennsylvania, published in 1905, William J. McKnight outlines some pertinent facts about the mountain lions that once were so prevalent throughout all of the Keystone State. McKnight claims that these magnificent beasts, also referred to as "panthers" in the old days, were "fully as strong as a bear, but were rather cowardly" [1] – an assessment not entirely in concert with stories about panther attacks that have sometimes come down to us via the highways of oral tradition, and which, in some cases, have even been recorded in other history books. Indeed, if all the verbally-preserved episodes are also accepted as having some legitimate truths behind them, rather than being rejected merely because they do not appear in some weighty leather-bound volume of "official" history, it is easy to conclude that, under the right conditions, panthers are not reduced to scared rabbits when encountering a man. In fact, just the opposite is true if someone is unfortunate enough to cross the path of a hungry lion with a fresh kill, or stumble upon a mother with newborn cubs.

Certainly among the things guaranteed to turn a mountain lion from a placid-looking pussy cat into a raging beast are the two situations just mentioned, and there were once, no doubt, many such stories that told of men being attacked for one of these two reasons. Such tales are hard to find today, except for those recorded in the many county histories that are kept in libraries, but a few of these stories and some accounts that have never been set down in print before are included in this essay just to give the reader an idea of how "rough and ready" the early settlers of these time-worn mountains must have been. And there is probably no better way to begin than to tell a story of old Sam Askey, that great panther hunter of Snow Shoe, Centre County.

Sam Askey's reputation as a slayer of many Pennsylvania panthers and wolves was well established throughout northern Centre and western Clinton County at one time, but those who counted him as a personal friend and who had heard him relate some of his hunting escapades claimed Askey's life would "compare with that of Daniel Boone or David Crockett" [2] Said to have been the slayer of sixty-four panthers and ninety-eight wolves just while living at Snow Shoe, Askey, during his lifetime of hunting, had several hand-to-hand encounters with panthers and bore the scars of these fights with him to his grave. No doubt the old hunter could tell a thrilling story about each of his panther wounds, and one such tale may just have been about the day he was ambushed by a lioness on Big Moshannon Mountain.

Askey, who died in 1857 at the "ripe" old age of eighty-one, was particularly fond of hunting on the Allegheny Mountains above Snow Shoe in that section of wild and untamed forest where the Big and Little Moshannon Creeks wind their way down to the West Branch of the mighty Susquehanna River. Spring, summer, winter, or fall, Askey could be found on these ragged slopes searching for deer, panthers, bears, or wolves to add to his long list of hunting trophies. However, it was during one cold winter day that the mighty hunter had one of his hand-to-hand fights with a panther.

A particularly good tracking snow had just fallen the night before, and Askey decided to take one of his best dogs hunting. It wasn't long before he found fresh tracks somewhere on the mountains between the two Moshannon Creeks. Since he was on a particularly difficult spot on the ridge, Askey decided to tether his dog to his body so as to keep the animal under control while he tried to follow the panther's tracks up the steep slope. Thinking he would release the dog once the hiking became easier, Askey finally made it to the top of the peak he called "the Big Moshannon Hill".

After reaching the brow of the ridge, the hunter and the little cur tethered to him approached a large rock that projected out over the trail. Just as they passed in front of the outcrop, a panther that lay concealed in an opening under it pounced upon the dog. The result was a writhing tangle of man, canine, and beast all rolling down the hill, with, in Askey's words, "sometimes the panther uppermost, sometimes the dog, and sometimes myself." [2]   Since the dog was tied to him with a slip knot, Askey managed to free himself, but the panther and dog rolled all the way down to the bottom of the slope, locked in a death struggle and, no doubt, growling and snarling at each other the whole time.

When the two animals reached level ground, the panther disengaged itself from the dog and raced up the nearest tree. This gave Askey time to retrieve his gun, which had fallen out of his grasp while he was rolling down the hill. Finding his rifle to be in good shape, the determined hunter spotted the panther up in the tree and brought the beast down with one well-directed shot.

Close inspection of the panther revealed that it was a female that had been nursing cubs, and so the fearless hunter decided he would make a first-hand inspection of the den under the rock from which the attack had come. The opening was just big enough to allow him to enter, and so he carefully squeezed into the dark hole. Much as he expected, there were four panther cubs hiding in the den, each about the size of a common house cat. Askey found them to be about as friendly as tame felines, and certainly friendlier than their mother, for he later noted that "after handling them for a short time they fondled on me like young kittens". [2]

However, the practical hunter and hardened veteran of countless chases had no intention of keeping the furry little bundles as pets. He must have killed them too, for he would later relate that the day's work had been hard and the bounties he received for the panthers' pelts were not enough to compensate him for the injuries that had been inflicted upon his dog. The faithful canine was permanently disabled by its terrible struggle with the mother panther, and, said Askey, 'was of no use to me afterwards." [2]

Sam Askey was certainly not the only one who had a hair-raising encounter with aggressive panthers here in Pennsylvania during the 1800's and early 1900's if an incident in Blackman's *History of Susquehanna County*, published in 1872, can be believed. According to Blackman's account, in 1806 a man named Asa Bradley built a log cabin in the unsettled wilderness around what was to become the present day town of New Milford. Bradley, his wife, and his children, were invited to stay with another pioneer family until the Bradley cabin was finished. Anxious to be in their new homestead, the Bradleys finally decided to move into the place. The walls and roof were constructed, but there was no front door. Nonetheless, it was a home, and they would no longer have to impose on their temporary hosts any longer, so the Bradleys hung a blanket over the opening where a front door would eventually be placed and moved in.

Sometime during their first night in the cabin, the family was awakened by loud squeals which came from a pig they had placed in a pen attached to the house. They didn't investigate the sounds since the squealing eventually died away, but the next morning when they went outside they discovered their pig was gone. After a brief search the Bradleys found the hog not too far from the house. The little porker had been partly devoured, and tracks all around the pig pen proved that the culprit was a panther. The Bradleys counted themselves lucky, despite the loss of the prized hog, for upon thinking about the matter they realized that if the pig had not been there for the panther's meal, then "what was to hinder the ravenous beast from entering the house for his supper?" [3]

Although the Bradleys were spared the horrors of a full-fledged panther attack, and so did not have to fend off the teeth and claws of such an intimidating beast, there were others who were not so fortunate over the years. Older folks around Blackwell, Tioga County, for example, still remember hearing stories when they were young about a local miner who was attacked and killed by a panther in earlier times. Details of the story seem to have been lost over the years, and this is what has probably happened to many other similar accounts as decades have passed, but this has not always been the case. Consider, for example, one striking episode from Lycoming County that occurred around the turn of the present century.

Many folks traveling north out of Salladasburg on Route 287 may never have paid much attention to a large stone sitting next to the right side of the highway just after they've passed through English Center. Peoples' eyes are naturally drawn instead to the inviting appearance of a neatly kept bed-and-breakfast lodge that sits further back from the road some distance behind the solitary rock. However, if a closer look is taken at the stone, the observer will note that fastened to it is a plaque that has an inscription upon it. The plaque has been exposed to the elements for so long that its black surface has weathered down in spots to bare metal of a bronze shade, the whole effect almost reminding one of a leopard's skin. In fact, if the inscription on the plaque is read, the reader will be surprised to learn that the commemorative plaque was placed there in memory of an incident involving one of the leopard's distant cousins.

The English Center marker is rather unique since it may be the only one in Pennsylvania that preserves the memory of a man being killed by one of the state's mountain lions. The inscription states the following:

> In memory of Dr. Frederick Reinwald.
> Dr. Reinwald was killed by a panther at Black's Creek,
> four miles northeast of this point, December 22, 1896,
> while on the way to visit a patient.
> An unusual example of the fortitude of pioneer physicians
> and the hazards faced in the performance of their duties.

There is no doubt that this incident actually happened and that the victim was an unfortunate doctor whose sense of duty was stronger than his concerns for his own safety. Such a man deserves to be remembered, and local legends supply a few additional details about the incident. "He went out toward

Liberty [Tioga County] with his horse and buggy to take care of some sick people, and he was killed by a black panther," offered one older native of the area. "That's the only one I ever heard about around here. I suppose the poor cat was hungry!" [4]

Although the color of the panther was probably tawny, the typical color of Pennsylvania mountain lions, instead of black, the good doctor's memory lives on in the folktales of Lycoming County. The unfortunate thing is that the Lycoming County physician was just in the wrong place at the wrong time, and without the means or chance to defend himself. However, in most cases the outcome of an encounter between humans and the big cats called panthers usually didn't end up with the mountain lions being victorious, a statement which is supported by another panther story from Centre County which tells of a mountain lion that attacked a man and paid the ultimate price for it. However, in this case it appears that, in the end, the panther eluded his killer after all.

"There was supposed to be a panther roaming the woods right close by here," said the valley native in a thick Pennsylvania Dutch accent as he was telling me the tales of the olden days one fine spring afternoon in 1989. "Oh, that was before I was born," continued the seventy-eight year old. "I heard about it when I was a kid. A neighbor, Samuel Styers, was an old, white-haired, man. He was up close to eighty years old, and he used to come out there and visit us. I didn't put too much stock in what he said because he was known as a big storyteller and a liar, but he told us that he had a son, and a panther attacked him one night.

"Later on he went out and he shot this panther along Woodward Mountain here. I always knew the names of the gaps in the mountain. Haines Gap is the one out here. Right out here where our reservoir is there's another break in the mountain called Young's Gap. And this panther was supposed to be making its home in Young's Gap here, and traveled west along the mountain toward Coburn. I was born in 1912, and I was about fifteen years old, I guess, when this old man Styers told me about that. So it must've been back in the 1800's, late 1800's, or maybe something like that.

"He wanted it mounted," continued the old story teller, "but he said he never had enough money to do it. He skinned it and gave it to a taxidermist, and the taxidermist mounted it. But they couldn't pay for it, so he didn't know what became of it. The taxidermist kept it." [5]

Perhaps it's just as well that the Styers' panther disappeared. Even stuffed ones seemed too lifelike at times for some people who weren't too sure about those teeth and claws that still looked threatening. Perhaps it was this uncertainty that gave birth to the old idea that stuffed panthers could come back to life at night and would roam the forests once again, just like they did when they were still alive. Such superstitions were also probably reinforced by the fact that dogs were often intimidated by these effigies. One such incident occurred during the early history of Susquehanna County, where it is recalled that during the early 1800's in Jackson Township there was a social gathering of some of the old pioneers of the area. Samuel Ard, who hosted the event, livened up the proceeding by exhibiting a stuffed panther, fully nine feet in length from the tip of its tail to the end of its nose. The taxidermist who had prepared the effigy had been so skillful that it was said that the panther "looked enough like life to frighten even dogs." [6] It probably frightened the women too, and no doubt it raised fears in many, women and men alike, that it would draw other panthers to it. Not something anyone who lived in those times would have wished for – particularly when it can surely be said that one of the credos of those days was that "the only good panther is a dead panther".

GUARDIAN OF THE TRAIL

Before it was known as Pennsylvania's "Black Forest", the region of northern Pennsylvania now comprised of most of Potter and Tioga counties was called the "Forbidden Land" by the first pioneers that ventured into what was then an area known only to the Indians and to the wild creatures that roamed through it at will. The story behind this unusual name is documented somewhat in the early historical records of the region, but there is a legendary component to the name's origin as well. However, this is a part of the story that has almost been forgotten over the years, but which deserves to be re-explored, not only to document once again the injustices that were once heaped upon the rightful owners of the land but also to find the possible source of one more ghost tale from the deep woods.

While William Penn, that benevolent founder of Pennsylvania, was alive, the Indians here were assured of fair treatment and kind respect. Rather than confiscate native American lands outright, like the Puritans of New England or the settlers of North Carolina, Penn insisted on paying the Indians for it. In fact, there was once a story told about Penn that preserves the popular conception, no doubt both then and now, of what type of man he was when dealing with native Americans. The tale relates that King Charles told the little Quaker that the land he had given him in the New World was England's by right of discovery.

"Well," said Penn, "just suppose a canoe full of savages should by some accident discover Great Britain. Would you vacate or sell?" [1] So unusual was this attitude in those days that one student of the times, alluding to the Quaker policy of refusing to utter an oath, either judicially or profanely, described Penn's "Great Treaty" with the Indians at Philadelphia in 1682 as "the only treaty never sworn to and never broken". [2] However, once the man the Indians called "Brother Onas" died, his policies toward them died as well, thereby setting the stage for the terrible Indian wars of later years.

The litany of broken promises and fraudulent agreements that were inflicted upon the Indians of Pennsylvania after William Penn died would fill volumes. Sometimes settlers were granted warrants to lands never purchased from the Indians, and even when purchases were made they were often done dishonestly. Probably the most famous deception on record was the notorious "Walking Purchase" of 1737 when it was agreed with the Delaware Indians living in Pennsylvania at that time that a purchase boundary would be limited by how far a man could walk in a day and a half. However, instead of walking normally, the athletes hired by government officials were instructed to run as fast as they could. Despite the shouted protests of the Delawares, the territory covered at the end of the day and a half was twice what the Indians had expected.

"No sit down to smoke, no shoot a squirrel, but lun, lun, lun all day long," [3] was the way one brave, 'R'-less as the other Delaware Indians until fully learning the white man's language, described the actions of the men who had covered the territory. But this protest was just as feeble as another made by an Iroquois chieftain in 1742 who protested that white people were settling on unsold Pennsylvania Indian lands daily, "and spoil our hunting". [4]

Eventually the attraction of white mens' trinkets and hardware no longer fascinated the Indians enough to persuade them to sell what they may have thought were merely the hunting rights to their lands. In the end, if an honest accounting were done, the amount the Indians received per acre of Pennsylvania territory was trivial, even for those days. In fact, it has been estimated that the actual value of the goods used to buy Indian lands, items like guns, coats, blankets, needles, pipes, shoes, knives, hatchets, scissors, combs, tin pots, and looking glasses, would probably come to less than a cent per acre.

Gradually some Indians began to see what was happening to their land and culture, much like the brave that one day sat down on a log beside Conrad Weiser , the Penn's highly respected Indian agent, and began to crowd him off of it. After several annoying nudges from the Indian, Weiser asked for an explanation.

"This," said the brave, "is what the whites did to the Indians. They lighted unbidden on our lands. We moved on; they followed. We still moved and they still followed. We are moving onward now, and they are following after. I will not push you from the log entirely, but will your people cease their crowding, ere we roll into the waters?" [5]

As time wore on, the Indians became more and more protective of their real estate, particularly that which was strategically important to them militarily, and of all the Indian trails that once existed in Pennsylvania, there was one that the Iroquois Confederacy considered especially important. This trail was known as the Forbidden Path because the Iroquois Six Nations Confederacy declared that no white man would ever set foot upon it. Also sometimes known as the Tioga Path, the trail was the "backdoor" to the Iroquois country. Skirting the southern boundaries of the Six Nations' tribal lands, this famous "warriors' path" ran from Tioga, Pennsylvania, through Painted Post and Salamanca, New York, eventually swinging back down into Pennsylvania where it passed through Genesee and then back into New York State.

A trail of such strategic importance could not be left unguarded, and so the Iroquois Confederacy designated the Seneca Nation, around Salamanca, New York, as their "Keepers of the Western Door". [6] Even peaceful Moravian missionaries, who were often the first white men to interact with many Indians, could not travel on the protected pathway. One such "Knight of the Cross" tried to do so one day in 1767, but was caught by a Seneca chief who demanded how he thought he could use "such an unfrequented road, which is no road for whites and on which no white man has ever come ? " [7] Finding that, after this, the Indians he came to teach were "not at all friendly to the cause of the Gospel", the devout man of God gave up his work here as a lost cause, and went west to find other souls that needed saving. [8]

It was this careful policing of the "Forbidden" Path that led the early settlers to call the entire area the Forbidden Land, a name that was eventually forgotten after the lands were purchased from the Indians near the end of the eighteenth century. However, the fact remains that this section of the state was one of the last to be explored and one of the last to be settled, and that is perhaps why we still have the old legend that came to be placed upon the area.

Up until now much of what's been covered in this essay may be a lot of "dry" history to most folks, but it has been necessary to cover it all in order to discover the origins of a ghostly tale that has been told and retold for over two-hundred years – a legend which still clings to the Forbidden Land if you just listen to the old folks who reach back into their memories to recall the story of the mysterious "Guardian of the Trail".

"There's a lake up there, over in the Forbidden Forest; the only lake, I guess, that Potter County has," recalled the Potter County farmer who had heard the story from an aged Seneca Indian. "Rose Lake, I think it is. Well, I don't know, the white man just never traveled through it. According to the French missionaries that were here with the Indians, they didn't travel through it - they went around it. Well, I can't give you it all, but the ghost of an Indian warrior comes out of the lake to keep people from traveling the trail through the Forbidden Land. The Indians talked about the ghost guarding the trail so that no white man could pass through. That's the gist of it."

After seemingly pondering the story a while, the farmer seemed to think it wasn't complete without some sort of explanation. "Why would they put a ghost story out?", he wondered, and then ended his tale with a final thought that is most likely the best explanation anyone can derive. "I think they used that to kind'a scare the early whites," he reasoned, and he's probably right. [9]

Due to the unquenchable greed of the early colonists, the people once known as the "red" race certainly had good reasons for wanting to keep the white one away from Indian lands. Initially it had probably seemed, to both whites and Indians alike, that there would be more than enough space for all. The mountains and ridges of Pennsylvania must have appeared to extend on forever to anyone gazing upon them for the first time in those days. In fact, the Indians' name for the Allegheny Mountains was *Tyannuntasacta* or "The Endless Hills" [10], but the whites were no less awed by what also appeared to them to be a limitless wilderness.

Through the greater part of the 1700's Pennsylvania was almost nothing but forest. In fact, a saying of the time was that "a squirrel could make its way from Philadelphia to Pittsburgh without ever leaving the trees". [11] With such a forested expanse it is not surprising that some sections of the state may have been harder to settle than others, but then the abundance of squirrels in some sections could have contributed to the lack of settlements as well. One such place may have been Clearfield County, and the other may have been the Forbidden Land.

Some historians indicate that the Indians avoided the Clearfield area for a number of reasons. The waterways through here were not navigable to any great extent, and so walking was the only way to pass through the region. However, during those early days there were a large number of wolves and panthers that made their homes here, making a journey by foot unduly hazardous. There was also a large rattlesnake population in this neighborhood, due to the huge squirrel population, which was maintained by the abundance of nuts and berries growing here.

Even by 1840, Clearfield county was still only partially settled, its population estimated to be just five people per square mile. After the lumbermen came and cleared the forest away at the turn of the century, nuts and berries didn't grow as profusely anymore. Without the food supply to sustain their former levels, the squirrel and rattler populations declined accordingly.

Similar to Clearfield County, the Forbidden Land section of Pennsylvania was tamed slowly too, not only because the Indians once restricted access to this part of Penn's Woods, but probably also because the wild animals that lurked here made it a forbidding place to be. But even these deterrents were not enough to keep the whites away, and the Indians must have realized that something more was needed to accomplish this.

The story about the ghostly guardian of the Forbidden Trail may have been the Indians' last desperate attempt to protect their native land. And, like a lot of legends, there may have even been some real episode upon which they based the story. There just may have been a warrior at one time, for example, who said that he would guard the Indians' lands even after he was dead. This motif of eternal purgatory would not be unusual; It is the basis for a number of famous legends including both "The Wandering Jew" and "The Flying Dutchman". If there ever was an Indian that uttered such an oath, then maybe he inspired others to recommit themselves toward protecting the lands of their ancestors.

Jim Jacobs of McKean County was an Indian who may have been carrying on just such a tradition. Around 1856, General Thomas Kane, who was the founder of Kane, McKean County, built a small log cabin of beech and maple logs, on what was later to be the site of Kane. The Colonel used the place as a hunting camp, but in those days a hunting camp was kept open for anyone's use when the owner wasn't there. However, General Kane, who believed the Indians, as original occupants of the country, had a moral right to the land, always kept his camp open for Jim Jacobs, an aged Seneca who seemed to be an aimless drifter. Although his purpose for being around was not clear, it was thought that Jacobs was placed here by the Senecas "to visit various places where treasure was hidden, and see if it was endangered by the encroachments of whites or uncovered by fire and windfall." [12]

Perhaps Jim Jacobs was carrying on an old Indian tradition which was the basis for the "guardian" legend. On the other hand, maybe the whites just made assumptions about Jim Jacobs' duties. Knowing there were silver deposits here, whose whereabouts were only known by the Indians, white settlers were always trying to find out a way to discover these lodes. They may have thought Jim Jacobs was around to insure that the deposits of precious metals stayed hidden. Whatever the truth may be, it's interesting to see that the white man also thought that there were watchmen assigned to this area by the Indians. Perhaps Jim Jacobs was the last of many 'guardians of the trail'.

Footnote:

If there are any ghosts guarding the Forbidden Land of the Indians, they must be mournful ones because they failed in their assigned task. In 1779 General John Sullivan and a huge contingent of Continental soldiers used the Forbidden Path to invade the Iroquois country and lay waste to its many Indian towns and settlements. It was a defeat from which the Indians never recovered. (See the story "Burned At The Stake" which appears in the author's *The Black Ghost of Scotia and More Pennsylvania Fireside Tales,* Volume II in this series of Pennsylvania mountain legends).

THAR'S GOLD IN THEM THAR HILLS

The phrase "Thar's gold in them thar hills" has perhaps been overused in many forms of popular entertainment over the years, but there really are gold and silver treasures to be found in the mountains of Pennsylvania if our legends are to be believed. Tales of hidden caches of silver and gold are common in many different sections of Pennsylvania, but the "northern tier" of counties, the former "Black Forest" region of Pennsylvania, seems to have more than its share of such stories. There are at least three tales of fabulous riches waiting to be found in the forests of the northern tier, and probably even more accounts than that if the matter were pursued. However, other parts of the state have produced similar legends as well, and it's interesting to compare them all.

One of the more popular Black Forest mysteries is set during the War of 1812. At this time supposedly over a million dollars worth of silver bars was buried near Keating Summit, McKean County. The old legend states that the British salvaged the treasure from the wreck of a Spanish galleon in the Bahamas, and then decided to ship it to a safe English port in North America. According to the rest of the legend, the expedition carrying the salvaged silver was led by a seaman known as Captain Blackbeard, who should not be confused with Edward Teach, the infamous pirate of the same nickname.

There were not many buccaneers that could claim the notoriety that Captain Teach achieved in the heyday of pirate ships. Exploits of the pirate with the luxuriant black beard were so well known in the early 1700's that the name "Blackbeard" became synonymous with piracy. In fact, Edward Teach the pirate probably inspired others to take up a similar way of life. At the very least, it seems that even as long as a hundred years after Teach's death in 1718 the thrill of piracy on the "high seas" still held an appeal for certain individuals. During the War of 1812, for example, there were seamen who, at the behest of the American government, were given the authority to raid British ships. The intent of these forays was to disrupt the British war effort against the United States, and for their trouble these "privateers" could keep anything of value they confiscated.

Bars of pure silver would have been a prize catch for any privateer, and so any British ship hauling such a treasure through American waters in 1812 would probably want to spend as little time at sea as possible. In fact, the existence of privateers around that time could explain why the McKean County legend goes on to state that Captain Blackbeard decided he would have better luck getting the salvaged silver bars into British hands if he were to dock at Baltimore and haul the silver overland. Determined to deliver the silver "booty" to British officials at any cost, and afraid to return with the loot to England because of a

Napoleonic blockade of the British Isles during that time, Blackbeard supposedly did lay anchor in Baltimore.

Here the legend continues, with Blackbeard fitting out an expedition that would follow the Susquehanna and Sinnemahoning rivers northward until it reached the British-controlled territories of New York. If, indeed, any such expedition was ever made, it most certainly seems it was trip that a seaman like Blackbeard would not forget.

A sailor who had never experienced the difficulties of backwoods travel in those days would have been totally unprepared for the super-human effort required to transport wagonloads of heavy silver bars over narrow mountain roads that were hardly worthy of the name. Any such journey would have taken many days of struggling through thickly-forested valleys, slogging around or through mosquito-infested swamps, and straining to get over high ridges that would have seemed like obstacles placed there by the Devil himself. None of these challenges would be anything like a veteran seaman had ever encountered during his many years at sea, and so this is probably why the legend claims that Blackbeard never completed his trip.

According to the tale, the intrepid sailor did manage to get as far as where Renovo, Clinton County, sits today, and then from there he took the twenty-three mile portage to the famous "Canoe Place" of the Indians, which we now call Port Allegany. Here Blackbeard, physically exhausted and uncertain of his chances of completing his mission, is said to have given up the attempt, deciding to bury the silver near an old saltlick that was a popular gathering spot for the many elk that inhabited the area. The unfortunate captain was never able to find his buried bars again, and it is these same bars, so says the legend, that still lie hidden in the wolf-haunted forests of McKean County.

Not to be outdone by its neighbor to the west, Potter County has two treasure stories that are just as appealing as McKean County's legend of the silver bars. The first Potter County legend describes another fortune in silver that is hidden near Inez, on that piece of territory known locally as "the Black Diamond". This Potter County silver was buried there, so says the legend, by the Jesuits, those early missionaries who Sipe has described as "true Knights of the Cross". [1]

"Two French traders and a Jesuit were gonna take a shipment of silver back up the Genessee," claimed one Potter County man who had heard the legend years ago. "They had got it off the Indians down here at the [Tiadaghton] trading post. They took it because the French wanted the silver. It was going to the French government in Canada. They were waylaid by bandits. They had buried the silver before they were waylaid, so the story goes. That's right over the hill from my house here, at Inez - the Black Diamond. But I imagine that there's been a million dollars spent looking for the damn thing. Yeah, it's an old story." [2]

Whenever treasure is mentioned, people tend to think not only of silver but also of gold, its metallic cousin, and a second Potter County legend tells of a fortune in gold that is said to be buried near Borie, in Summit Township. Near here, says the popular tale, a party of French Canadian voyageurs and priests decided to hide several kegs of gold coins they were transporting from New Orleans to Montreal sometime in the 1690's. The Seneca Indians were considered too great a threat to their expedition, and so the voyageurs are said to have resorted to the same plan as that of McKean County's Captain Blackbeard: bury the gold and come back for it later.

According to the legend, the voyageurs never did come back, and the coins are said to be there yet, buried near a large rock. Supposedly the Frenchmen marked the spot, so they could easily find it later, by chiseling a mark onto the stone. The mark they chose was a cross, and "the cross on the rock" was once a familiar landmark in the Borie area.. No one knows where it is today.

However intriguing the tale of the voyageurs' gold, it has never achieved the popularity, nor spurred the quests, that another northern tier legend of lost gold has over the years. By far the most famous fortune of the northern tier is the wagonload of gold bullion that unaccountably disappeared one June day in 1863. The tale of this lost gold shipment has probably created more weekend treasure hunters in Pennsylvania than all the state's other treasure stories combined. The legend has been kept alive for over one-hundred years by the residents of Elk and Cameron Counties, who remember the fuss the incident caused during the Civil War, and who have seen a steady stream of fortune seekers flow into the area ever since.

"They were shipping gold from Pittsburgh up around by Saint Marys and down the Susquehanna, during the Civil War, by mule train in an Army force," recalled the man who had heard the tale from the time he was a boy. "It come up out of Pittsburgh. To where it come from to Pittsburgh, I don't know. Maybe they stole it from the rebels down there. They were coming up around what they called the safe route, away from the southern troops in southern Pennsylvania, to have it minted at the Philadelphia mint. The only safe route was the northern route from Pittsburgh up through the Alleghenies and back down the Susquehanna. A bunch of bandits, or a bunch of roughnecks or hoodlums, or whatever you want to call them, found out about it.

"They [the Army troops] bivouacked at Saint Marys, and they left Saint Marys, coming over here to Driftwood, where they could float it down the Susquehanna by boat. And between Driftwood and Saint Marys they were attacked by these ruffians or outlaws, or whatever you wanta call it, and they were killed, and the gold was made off with. The gold disappeared. One team of mules and one Army sergeant, negro Army sergeant, ended up in Driftwood. But the Army come and got him, and he could never remember what happened as far as anybody knew. But the Army come and got him, as the story goes; and he died in service. The government has hunted for that shipment of gold ever since.

"But according to that old Army sergeant, he said the gold had been buried when they found out they were gonna be attacked. That they took the horse and the mules and the wagon that had the gold on and they took it and hid it. So the gold has never turned up in the records of anyplace, and Uncle Sam is still hunting it. Years ago they used to send a team in here about every two or three years to try to figure it out. I imagine they still got a record because it was Army gold, and the Army never forgets anything. National Geographic was in here. They was gonna run an article, but they never did. I think they got in touch with the Army command and it was squashed.

"I've heard it [the story] ever since I was a kid in Emporium; and it's over there at the bar; the whole damn story's printed out on a newspaper that was printed in Clearfield, I guess, back at that time. And there used to be a little library at Sterling Run. That's up above Driftwood. It had, when I was a kid, it had a whole story printed on the wall about this thing. And then in Driftwood, behind the old bar across from the railroad station, the whole thing was there. I heard about it ever since I was big enough to walk because Dad was an engineer on the railroad. We lived in Emporium, and there was all kinds of stories when I was growing up in Emporium about people hunting for the gold up on the mountain." [2]

There are those who still search for the lost gold shipment, not only because of the amount of money involved but also because there is little doubt that the incident actually happened. Despite the fact that the famous sharp-shooting "Bucktail" Regiment, so-called because of the tails of buck deer they wore in their caps, came from this area during the Civil War, there were still many "Copperheads" in these same counties at the time the gold shipment was ambushed. These southern sympathizers would probably have been only too happy to steal some of Uncle Sam's gold, especially if it would have enriched the coffers of the Confederacy, not to mention their own coffers. If the gold shipment of 1863 was ambushed, it may have been a robbery committed by a band of these Confederate allies.

Besides the fact that there were people in the area that may have had a motive for committing the robbery of the gold shipment, there was also an obvious path over which the gold may have been transported. Long before the turbulent times of the 1860's there was a military road through this same section of the Black Forest which dated back to the 1750's, the time of the French and Indian War. This road ran from present-day Lock Haven, through Renovo, Driftwood, and Emporium, and on to the Allegheny. This route generally corresponds to the route said to have been taken by the gold shipment and was "much used by early settlers" [3]

Despite the legendary claims that the gold has never been found, there are some who think otherwise. Up in Emporium there was once a lot of talk about "the millionaire", an eccentric who had come to town with nothing, but somehow got enough money to build a large hotel. However, the large structure was misplaced as far as everyone else was concerned. Situated back in the mountains near a remote water tower that railroad trains stopped at to take on water, the hotel was a "fish out of water" since there was never anyone else around to patronize the place. Popular opinion was that the eccentric innkeeper had money to burn if he could do something as absurd as he had done, and the only apparent way he could have gotten that kind of money, most people thought, was to have found the lost gold shipment. Opinion didn't change much after the man died, for stories surfaced claiming that the old boy had requested that some of the gold be buried with him in his grave.

Speculative at best, the story of the millionaire and his hotel do nothing to prove or disprove the tale about the lost gold shipment. There are, however, parts of the lost gold shipment story which are similar to tales related in other parts of the state. Although these other accounts may merely be based on the same legendary elements which are embedded in the story of the lost gold shipment of Elk and Cameron Counties, these similarities, on the other hand, may be an indication that the incidents recounted in the old legends are based on actual events.

There are at least two other tales that have details similar to that of the Elk County story. The first account was once popular in the Allegheny Mountains around the community of Snow Shoe in Centre County. Here it was once believed that six barrels of gold were hidden away in the mountains near a hotel called the Mountain House in 1864. Reason for the concealment, said the story, was that many bank directors were in a panic. They were afraid that the Confederate army had a good chance of taking over Pennsylvania. Rather than let their gold fall into the hands of the Confederacy, the banks in the southern parts of the state decided to ship their gold reserves to safer ground in northern Pennsylvania.

What is certain today is that the Mountain House was built in 1859 by the Bellefonte and Snow Shoe Railroad Company, the same corporation that laid out the village of Snow Shoe itself in 1858. John Essington, landlord of this remote wayside inn around the time of the Civil War, was one of several innkeepers who eventually helped establish the lodge's reputation as the premier hotel of the town. However, despite the fact that the inn was once a well-frequented layover for travelers, the six barrels of gold said to be buried near the place have reportedly never been found.

Another similar story of lost Civil War gold has remained a popular Adams County tale since the time of the great conflict between the North and the South. Scars of that great struggle have not faded away completely over the years, nor have the stories that grew out of it, and one of the ugliest scars left upon the region was the burning of the town of Chambersburg by Confederate forces in 1864.

"I know they [the Confederate army] robbed Chambersburg, and they burnt it," recalled the old farmer from the South Mountains. "The reason they burnt it wasn't just for pure hate. They done it because the north burnt one of their towns. That's a true story; and they got even. It was Civil War. Well, they were shipping it [gold] from out of Chambersburg, east. That's where it would be coming; and they hid it in the mountains somewhere. I think it was Yankee gold. The south was in Chambersburg, see; and they hid it to get away from them. Then they got killed or something.

"Well, I have an idea where it is - around Cashtown. It's between Cashtown and Fayetteville. There at Caledonia. It's Caledonia, east. That would be from Caledonia, east - not from Fayetteville. That would be the old National Pike coming through there, and that's all growed up in trees. That was an important highway. It's been there for a long time. The road has been changed some. But, anyhow, they hid it [the gold], and they never come back or something. It's there. I believe it's there. But the road is indistinguishable, and they hid [the gold] in the mountains somewhere. I think it's there, really." [4]

The burning of the Franklin County town of Chambersburg by the Confederate forces of McCausland and Johnston on July 30, 1864 was one of the low points of the Civil War for the residents of southern Pennsylvania. Undaunted by their defeat at Gettysburg the year before, the rebel army under General Jubal Early had orders to burn the town of Chambersburg if the residents of the town refused to pay a ransom of $100,000 in gold. Unable to come forth with that kind of money, the residents of Chambersburg had to stand by in disbelief as their homes went up in flames.

First-hand accounts of the episode describe the way citizens of the town were stopped on the street by Confederate soldiers and robbed of all their valuables. The relief of those citizens who were fortunate enough to avoid being robbed on the streets was often short-lived. Other accounts of the raid tell how the rebels plundered homes of silverware, jewels, clothes and anything else of value, oftentimes putting the house to the torch after stripping away the wealth within.

The citizens of Chambersburg were not exactly strangers to the visits of an invasion force. During the fall of 1862 Jeb Stuart's cavalry raided the town, and in the summer of 1863 General Robert E. Lee's troops, on their way to a meeting with destiny at a peaceful country town called Gettysburg, had swept through the area, robbing Chambersburg's farmers of wagons, horses, and grain.

It was only natural, given the experiences of invasions by Confederate forces on two other occasions, that with the threat of yet a third invasion in 1864 the people of Franklin County would take whatever measures they could to avoid losing their valuables. This contingency seemed especially appropriate since no Union troops appeared to be forthcoming to do battle with the rebels. With the notice that Jubal Early's troops had crossed the Potomac, the farmers and merchants of Chambersburg began to remove their livestock and things of value from the area.

Residents of the town knew that their actions were sound ones. *"That farmers should send away their horses, and merchants their goods, at the approach of the enemy, is not only natural, but eminently wise and proper,"* noted one citizen who experienced the raid first-hand. *"Allowing them to remain at home, without the ability to defend them from capture, would be giving aid and comfort to the enemy."* [5]

Given the mass withdrawal of valuables that occurred in Franklin County prior to the invasion of 1864, it would seem just as natural for the banks in that area to remove their money and gold as well. This is, no doubt, just what happened, and such actions are similar to what could have prompted the shipments of gold referred to in the legends of Elk and Centre Counties. The question remains, however, as to whether or not any of the treasures mentioned in these old legends were ever found. If not, then some lucky person may yet do so someday. It would not be the first time someone got rich by finding one of Pennsylvania's lost treasures.

Two Montour County men found one such jackpot on a November day in 1884. Their good luck was so amazing that details of their windfall appeared in the *Berwick Independent,* dated November 27, 1884. The account may offer some encouragement for today's treasure hunters:

One Saturday afternoon of last week while Frank Lewis and Jack Gearhart were digging fern roots on the island, three miles below Danville, they unearthed an iron box which was completely covered with rust. To their utter astonishment, they found it filled with gold and silver coin of a very ancient date. Mr. Kinter (a railway agent), being an expert, took charge of the counting, and after 10 hours of steady work he had the money counted out in $1,000 piles amounting to $47,000. Mr. Kinter assures Messrs. Gearhart and Lewis that by strictly adhering to their usual temperate habits, they can lay by the shovel and hoe for the rest of their lives and live in ease and comfort.

The general supposition is that the money was placed there by Captain Kidd sometime in the 16th century. Being hard-pressed on the Chesapeake Bay by other pirates, he entered the Susquehanna River and sailed up Crook's Riffles, which at the time formed part of the island. In order to save the money he buried it. [6]

Perhaps other Pennsylvanians will once again be just as lucky as Mr. Lewis and Mr. Gearhart. It's hard to imagine the excitement that accompanied the discovery of the hidden box of coins in 1884, but the interest generated then would pale in comparison to the stir the event would create now. Today such a discovery would receive both newspaper and television coverage, prompting a whole host of treasure hunters to dust off their metal detectors and head for the hills, seeking out the lost gold and silver fortunes of Pennsylvania's romance-filled mountains.

CAMPBELL'S LEDGE

Throughout the entire Wyoming Valley of Luzerne County there are few landmarks more prominent than Campbell's Ledge. Towering over the North Branch of the Susquehanna opposite the town of Exeter along Route 92, this imposing rock face rises to a height of 1,364 feet above sea level and almost 600 feet above the valley below. The size and age of such an enormous cliff are enough to make it historically noteworthy in its own right, and there has been much written about the place over the years. However, there still seems to be a bit of uncertainty about how the cliff got its name. In fact, history and legend have preserved different versions about the origins of the ledge's title, but in this case it would appear that legend, rather than history, supplies us with the true story.

Early historical records of the Wyoming Valley do contain many graphic details of the numerous Indian raids that were inflicted upon the settlers of that area during the Revolutionary War. It was during one of these bloody episodes, so says the old legend, that an event so remarkable occurred that it prompted the survivors to rename the prominent geological landmark along present-day Route 92. On the other hand, many scholars have claimed that there are no hard facts in the historical records that uphold the legendary explanation, and so the academics have dismissed the legend in favor of their own conclusions.

As it sometimes happens in these matters, once a popular historical explanation is given a blessing by the experts it becomes hard to displace, especially when there is no historical evidence to support alternate ideas, especially those of the legendary kind. With this thought in mind, it is easy to see why historians willingly accepted the conclusions of their predecessors when it came to the history behind the name of the famous ledge in the Wyoming Valley. However, unmindful of the "hard, cold facts", the old legend refuses to die. It is still a popular tale, told and retold by the descendants of those who settled the valley during those times when blazing cabins filled the skies with smoke and the blood of massacred settlers colored the soil red.

Despite their differences of opinion, history and legend do agree on one thing, and that is that the Wyoming Valley's Indian troubles served as the basis for the naming of Campbell's Ledge. However, the two diverge quite remarkably at that point, with history claiming that the name of the ledge can be traced to the pen of a peaceful poet, and legend stating that the landmark's title is rooted in those days of Indian warfare when the scalping knife and fire brand were the scourge of the Wyoming Valley.

Out of all the terrible incidents that occurred in the Wyoming Valley during the Revolutionary War, probably the most infamous was the massacre that took place almost two years to the day after the signing of the Declaration of Independence. It was on the third day of, July, Independence month, 1778, that the infamous Wyoming Massacre took place, resulting in a widespread exodus of settlers throughout the Pennsylvania frontier – a panic that was later remembered as "The Great Runaway". The slaughter at Wyoming was an incident that, according to one historian, "shocked the world and brought deep sympathy for the American cause". [1]

The historian's statement was a true one, for news of the incident at Wyoming did travel across the sea, and it struck a particularly sensitive chord with a Scottish poet named Thomas Campbell. Campbell was so moved by the stories of the sufferings of those who were victims of the Indians' wrath at Wyoming that he composed a poem that captured the scenes of the event in words that only a poet can produce. In fact, Campbell's "Gertrude of Wyoming" became a very famous rhyme – so famous, in fact, that his heroine Gertrude became as closely identified with Wyoming as the poet Longfellow's heroine Evangeline became associated with Acadia.

Historians, aware of peoples' tendency to associate Thomas Campbell with the story of the Wyoming Massacre, took the association a step further and assumed that Campbell's Ledge was named after the poet as well. However, this is an assumption that is incorrect, at least according to the legend that says an unrecorded historical event is the basis for the name of the prominent cliff.

"You could see it from where we lived. You could see this ledge, you know, in the distance, from where we lived," recalled the native son of the Wyoming Valley who knew the area legends quite well..

"There was the story about Campbell," continued the former Pittston resident who had heard the story from his parents when he was just a young lad. "[Campbell] was in charge of a militia or something, you know. He was a scout, around the time of the French and Indian Wars, [and] he was scouting all along the top of that mountain. And they [the Indians] came across him. They were camped there. Whether he discovered one of their camps, or what, they started chasing him. They were gonna kill him. They had horses and he outran them. He rode along and the only chance he had was to get into the river.

" Well, at the time the river was really high. It ran under the ledge. It's pretty far from there now, you know. But he leaped off the ledge on his horse. His horse broke its neck when it hit the water. It was a pretty high jump. His horse got killed, but he survived that. Well, he was in the river then, and there was no way they could catch him, because at the time that Susquehanna River had a hell of a current. He was okay. [He] just escaped along the river and got back to the settlement and warned them that the Indians were in that area. I never heard anything about him after that. That's how it got its name, Campbell's Ledge." [2]

111

Perhaps one of the reasons that historians prefer to ignore this old account that claims to be the basis for the naming of Campbell's ledge is because the story does indeed have legendary qualities. Typical of any legend, the tale of the Indian scout Campbell's fantastic escape from certain death is not all that unique, apparently having a tendency to travel from one place to another. However, unlike other legends that often have to migrate thousands of miles before they find a second home, this story lazily settled on a red sandstone ledge of eight-hundred feet in height located only about eighteen miles south of Campbell's Ledge.

This other impressive ledge is today known as Tillsbury Knob, but it was formerly called Rampart Rocks because of a battle of that name that was fought here during the struggle between Connecticut and Pennsylvania settlers for control of the region during the last quarter of the eighteenth century. The old legend of how Rampart Rocks got a new name was passed on to me by another lover of the old-time tales; a migrant himself, he was living in Phillipsburg, Pennsylvania at the time I interviewed him..

According to the old gentleman's legendary account, Tillsbury Knob was named for an early settler, named Tillsbury, who, in the early 1700's, rode his horse over the ledge to escape Indians. "Knowing the way Indians drove buffalo over cliffs out west, they probably thought it was a good place to trap a white man," commented the former Wilkes-Barre resident. "His horse was impaled on a tree, which saved his life. He was able to crawl down out of the tree and then swim safely to Nanticoke." [3]

Although the historical record of the many Indian battles in the Wyoming Valley would agree that incidents like those preserved in the Tillsbury Knob or Campbell's Ledge legends could have been based on real events, it seems like too much of a stretch to believe that two very similar fantastic escapes such as these could have happened so close geographically. One account just may be a distorted version of the other localized to a different section. However, the doubt still remains as to which account, if one is indeed based on fact, is the true one. It's a question that can't be answered with any certainty today, but it's interesting to note that there are, indeed, other places in the state also said to be named after similarly remarkable but unverifiable events..

Although it's a bit of a digression, there's another account from the Wyoming Valley that shows just how difficult it often is to put any stamp of authenticity on a legend. This episode also involves another Wyoming Valley landmark, a small hillock located directly across from Tillsbury Knob and known locally as Honeypot Knob. The unusual name comes from the fact that on the knob's peak is a bowl-like depression in which honeysuckle vines grow profusely during the summer months. It was below this fragrant and beautiful site, according to local legend, that the so-called "Grasshopper War" occurred. However, no historical records mention such a battle, and details about it are preserved only in legendary accounts. Although the legends agree in most respects, they do have one problem, and that is they don't agree on where the struggle took place.

According to the Wyoming Valley version of the legend, one summer day some Shawnee Indian women and their children were peacefully gathering fruit from bushes and trees which grew at the foot of a small elevation that the early white settlers would later call Honeypot Knob. Not too far away a group of Delaware Indian women and their children were picking fruit as well. No doubt such a scene would have been a pleasant one: warm summer breezes filling the air with the fragrance of honeysuckle flowers, dusky Indian maidens busily picking berries from blackberry or huckleberry bushes, and laughing Indian children finding delight in even the simplest of nature's creations.

At this moment one of the children found a large grasshopper and began playing with it. Another child, attracted by the bug, tried to play with it also, and a squabble began. Soon the mothers were involved, and an argument started over which group had territorial rights to this particular area. Then more children and women joined the fight until they were all in the fray. At this point the warriors returned from a peaceful hunting trip, and they immediately jumped into the melee to protect their squaws and children.

The contest was a long and bloody affair, and, according to the legend, when the sun finally sank behind the hills the last rays of sunlight fell upon a battlefield strewn with corpses, mostly comprised of the Shawnee's finest warriors. It was as a result of this victory, claims the legend, that the Delawares were able to expel the Shawnees from the valley. [4]

As intriguing as this story is, it seems to have the same problem as the Tillsbury Knob story in that it can't quite decide where it should call home. Up in Juniata County, for example, there is another legend that claims the Grasshopper War for Juniata County. This folktale relates that the Grasshopper War was actually a battle fought between the Delaware and Tuscarora tribes on the banks of Licking Creek near Mifflintown.

Although the story is an intriguing one, the tale of the Grasshopper War is also a curious example of a legend being relocated to a different spot from where it may have actually happened. After a relocation such as this it is difficult, if not impossible, to determine where the original event may have occurred. This, in turn, casts doubt on the certainty of whether or not the event happened at all - it may have just been a "tall tale" of that day and age. All that can be done in such cases is to look at whether such an event was possible given the historical facts, and this is exactly how we'll look at the legend of Campbell's Ledge.

Anyone who reads the history of the Wyoming Valley will find that two-hundred and sixty years ago, in 1737, Campbell's Ledge overlooked the site of an Indian village known as *Assarughney*. It was probably not a place where a white man would have wanted to tarry very long, since many residents of the settlement were Delaware Indians who had been forced off their homelands and pushed to the west as a result of being cheated by the infamous "Walking Purchase". This deceitful scheme by the heirs of William Penn alienated the Delaware against Pennsylvania more than any other misdeeds on the part of the white man. It was, they said, a deciding factor in their decision to take up arms against Pennsylvania during the French and Indian War that would flare up twenty years later.

In addition to providing a home base for the many Delaware Indians that lived here, and who most probably harbored an intense dislike of whites in general, *Assarughney* was sometimes a layover for Indian warriors just passing through. These braves would most likely not have been all that friendly either. Many were probably in raiding parties traveling along the Great Warriors Path, the famous Indian trail, from Tioga to Shamokin and points south, which passed directly beneath Campbell's Ledge. Such war parties would be in a belligerent mood, preparing themselves to do battle with other Indian tribes in the Carolinas.

The prominent ledge probably invoked strong emotions in the Indians when they saw it, perhaps because it would have been a reminder of their many wars with their enemies. This would have made it a special place for them, and it apparently was not just an ordinary landmark to the early white settlers either. In fact, the whites actually had a practical use for the place according to early records. These accounts state that the first settlers in the area referred to the ledge as Dial Rock since it served as a timepiece of sorts for them. Usually the stone face of the cliff near the summit is gray and somewhat in shadow, but at precisely midday the rays of the sun fall on the shadowy face of the ledge signaling the noon hour just as clearly as the hands on a clock.

Even if the Indians didn't view the ledge in any special way, they certainly did not consider the Wyoming Valley merely another place to live. They fought the whites harder for no land than they fought for the Wyoming Valley. The whole area was a place that the Shawanese, Nanticokes, and Delaware Indians must have thought of as their paradise. Game of all sorts was particularly abundant in this unspoiled Eden, and the streams and river contained plenty of fish like trout and shad. Crops of corn and squash grew well in the valley, as did wild grapes and wild berries of all types. In fact, it might be said that conditions here were as close as an Indian could get to his "Happy Hunting Ground" without actually dying and going on to the next world. It is little wonder, then, that when white men began to move into the Wyoming Valley it became the scene of many bloody Indian battles and massacres.

The first massacre that occurred in the Wyoming Valley took place in October of 1763 when one hundred and thirty-five Delaware Indians killed about twenty settlers who were at work in their fields – a slaughter that signaled the opening of what was to be a campaign of terror. Thinking they had been promised the Wyoming lands by the Six Nations as their permanent hunting ground and place of abode, the Delaware learned that the great Iroquois Confederacy had sold the land out from under them, and they meant to exact their revenge. Other major massacres followed in 1778, 1779, and in 1780, but numerous others occurred throughout the valley at various times between 1763 and 1778. In the years 1772 and 1773, in particular, there was a widespread fear of attack and the people lived in forts.

Such conditions are the stuff of which tall tales and legends are made, but they also can be the setting for actual events which take on legendary proportions. It is in this "gray area" which the legend of Campbell's Ledge seems to fall. It may just be a tall tale, but it has enough of an historical ring to it that at least one of the earliest Wyoming Valley historians included the account in his history of the valley.

"There is a wild legend which has given the name to this ledge," states George Peck. "A man named Campbell was pursued by the Indians. He had taken refuge in the ravines of this mountain, where are many fine living springs, and where thick foliage afforded a safe shelter. But the fierce Red Men are on his track. He is an old enemy, and is singled out for special torture. He knows his fate if taken. He tries every path that winds out into the deeper forest, but without success. He is hemmed in like the roe by the relentless wolves. But he does not hesitate; he springs forward to the verge of the hanging rock. One glance behind him shows him that escape is utterly hopeless. The shouts of the savages are heard as they rush upon their prey. With a scream of defiance, he leaps into the friendly arms of death." [5]

One final fact should be mentioned that may interest those who are interested in the odd and the old events of times gone by – a fact that indirectly supports the theory that Campbell's Ledge was named from a singular event that occurred there. In those days of Indian warfare there were many brave men, but there were some men whose courage and deeds of valor were so outstanding that they were awarded a special degree of respect. One such man was Samuel Brady, Indian fighter and frontier scout from Lycoming County.

An early biographer of Sam Brady states that Brady's very name was enough to quiet the fears of settlers' children when they were assured that Captain Brady and his rangers were on watch. Sam Brady was indeed regarded by the Indians as one of their greatest enemies. Once when they had actually captured him they prepared special torments, feeling sure that he would be able to endure more pain than any captive they had ever tortured. However, at the last possible moment Brady was able to break away. He, too, was pursued by warriors, and in order to escape had to make a fantastic leap of twenty-five feet or more across a chasm between two bluffs. The Indians, believing no man could jump like this, concluded that Brady was a wild turkey and had flown across. They then carved a picture of a wild turkey's foot onto the rock where Brady had landed. To this day the spot is known as Brady's Hill.

There is also a Brady's Creek in Allegheny County, named after the same Sam Brady, and other such locations, named after other early idols, could also be mentioned. But the point is that during those times landmarks were often named after exceptional individuals whose larger than life deeds at those spots were particularly significant to the early settlers of that area. Campbell's Ledge may be another such place, but in this case the legend, if true, raises only doubts and leaves us with a shadowy figure who would have been considered a hero of that day and age.

View of Campbell's Ledge, Luzerne County

CAST INTO STONE

Sometime, in the years ahead, there may be a reader of these lines who will want to try to collect the old-time legends and folktales similar to the ones recorded in the present volume and in the other volumes of this series. Although the individual may have some luck in their endeavors, time is the enemy of such a commendable task; the rate at which these relics of a bygone age are disappearing increases with the passing of each year. Tellers of the old episodes are now "up in their seventies" or older, and the younger generations seem less inclined to pass the accounts on to their own children. Nonetheless, it does seem likely that there will always be sanctuaries for the narratives somewhere in our mountains – places where the tales have already survived for so long, not only because they are interesting but also because the people there seem to appreciate them more. If that is true, then one of these sanctuaries will be the hills and valleys of southern Pennsylvania.

Every year thousands of tourists drive through the south central part of our state on their way to see the National Military Park at Gettysburg, and it's probably safe to say that almost none of them realize that they are driving through that section of ridges Pennsylvanians call the South Mountains. Almost everyone has heard of the Blue Ridge Mountains of Virginia and North Carolina, that rugged stretch of Appalachia where tales of moonshiners, hardy mountaineers, and unsurpassed mountain vistas await the visitor. But Pennsylvania's South Mountains, even though they are the northernmost extension of the Blue Ridge chain, are not as widely heralded as their southern cousins. Nonetheless, these Pennsylvania hills abound with the same kind of legendary lore. In fact, it's probably fair to say that the South Mountains still rank among the most legend-shrouded peaks in the entire state. Tales of ghosts, witches, and Indians can still be heard here today in the Cumberland Valley, told just as they were a hundred years ago; and although there are many such stories awaiting the collector, none can probably tweak the imagination more than the legend of the Indian sentry of the South Mountains.

Down in Franklin County there is a prominent elevation lying among the South Mountains that was known locally at one time as Caledonia Mountain. The small ridge that looms over Thaddeus Stevens' old iron furnace is known today as Rocky Mountain, which is more in keeping with the condition of the surface of the land on the mountain top. Located in Michaux State Forest, Rocky Mountain frowns down upon Caledonia State Park, and also upon the site of the old Graffenburg Inn, that ancient hostelry that was once a favorite stopping place for travelers passing through the South Mountains. Destroyed by fire some twenty or thirty years ago, the Graffenburg Inn is now only a name found in the history books, a fate that at least guarantees the old hostelry some measure of immortality. Unfortunately, the same cannot be said for the Indian warrior whose stone face on top of Rocky Mountain gazes stoically out over the Cumberland Valley.

Many hikers have undoubtedly walked past the silent sentinel numerous times. The Appalachian Trail lies right next to the unusual stone formation, but probably very few passersby have ever even noticed a face on the rocks. There are, in fact, supposed to be two such profiles on the mountain, one the result of glacial action or some other natural weathering process, and the other sculpted by the hand of man. The face formed naturally is the one associated with the curious legend that is said to have come down to us from the Indians that once lived here. The natural likeness, no doubt, prompted someone, perhaps an old stonecutter, to sculpt the other face into the rock.

One reason hikers miss the faces may be that there are more obvious attractions for those who make the steep trek up the mountain. Fine views of eastern Franklin County and western Adams County can be enjoyed from the trail, and near here are some lofty rock ledges known as Buzzards Peak where buzzards can be seen on occasion. Why the buzzards picked this particular spot to frequent is not exactly clear, but perhaps they were drawn here in the same manner they were attracted to the number of dead lying on the battlefield after the battle at Gettysburg.

It seems that once buzzards are drawn to a choice spot they tend to stay there, as do their subsequent offspring. It is said that that is why there are so many buzzards to be seen even today at the Gettysburg battlefield. Others say the buzzards were always there, and that the battle had nothing to do with attracting them from somewhere else. However, if the explanation for the presence of so many buzzards at Gettysburg is true, then the explanation for the buzzards that make their home on Caledonia Mountain could lie in the legend about this place, if the story has any basis in fact. But the buzzards do seem to get scarcer every year, just like the number of people who know about Caledonia Mountain's Indian face, and the legend behind it that reads like a Greek tragedy.

Probably the main reason that hikers never see the stone face is that they never look for it. Very few people know about the legend today, and that's probably because it's so old, its origins rooted in the misty annals of the mountains prior to the time when any white men had even entered this area. The legend, which still surfaces from time to time in some villages and valleys of Franklin County, recalls the time when the Munsees, a branch of the Delaware Indians that was also known as the "wolf tribe", could be found in the forests around Caledonia. The Munsees and the powerful Iroquois confederacy known as the Six Nations were, during this period, reaching the end of what had been years of struggle over control of native lands throughout various parts of the state. This seemingly endless warfare had taken its toll upon the Munsees so that their numbers, and the lands they controlled, were dwindling.

Eventually, so states the legend, the tiny band of Delawares was pushed westward until one day they found themselves in a small valley to the west of the ridge we now call Rocky Mountain. Knowing that their Iroquois enemies were following them, the Munsees took extra precautions to ensure the safety of their families. Every night they would post a lookout on the mountain in whose shadow they were encamped. The sentry was, in the words of one early account, to "shoot an arrow, marked by a knot of buckskin, into the lodge of his brethren if he saw the hated warriors of the Six Nations approach by day, and to set fire with his flints the piles of brush if he discovered them coming by night".[1]

On one particular night, "the camp went to sleep, and as [the sentry] was doing the watch an Indian maiden, who was a warrior's daughter, of the tribe, come out and said she'd set with him," claimed a South Mountains farmer who recalled the rest of the narrative for me one day when we were driving out to Caledonia to see if we could find the interesting face on the mountain,.

"He told her it's not a woman's place to be with a warrior when he's guarding," continued the old gentleman. "So she said, 'Never mind. There'll be two of us to watch and hear.'

"And he still protested, but she insisted in the ways of a woman, and, you know, they'll get their way. So she stayed with him. Well, they fell asleep together instead of listening and watching, and the Iroquois come into the camp that night and wiped out everybody except this girl's father and the shamus, or witch doctor. So the only ones that were left were those two. But actually the tribe was literally wiped out there." [2]

Another source for the legend described the attack in more romanticized terms, noting that the arrows of the Iroquois fell "like hail from an overcast sky", and that the invaders "buried their tomahawks and battle axes in men, women, and children until the lodge was quiet as before – only that the sleep of the braves was deeper now than then".[1] All accounts agree on what supposedly happened next, however, and that was that the girl's father and the witch doctor realized that the sentry had not done his duty, and they went looking for him. He had been mortally wounded and was near death when they found him on the mountaintop. Next to him was the body of the young maiden, her head split open by a tomahawk.

"Her father was very sad about his daughter being killed, but he didn't have any animosity toward the warrior boy that should have been watching the trail," continued the old farmer, as he tried to remember the story as best as he could. "But the shamus, he was extremely angry, and he cast the boy's spirit into those rocks. And henceforth and forevermore he shall watch the pass, and he shall never rest. His eyes shall be open, but he won't be able to see and his ears will be there, but he won't be able to hear, and he shall always watch the pass." [2]

Today the old legend of the sentry of the South Mountains seems like a fairy tale, but there are historical truths embedded in the ancient account, and a pursuit of those truths reveals some interesting possibilities as far as what the origin of the story might have been. The search for the facts behind the legend begins in the times before the white man came to America. For centuries prior to the appearance of white men there had been a history of intertribal warfare between the numerous Indian tribes of Pennsylvania. There was not continual warfare, but it occurred frequently enough that the times of peace were appreciated and enjoyed. Mary Jemison, known as "the white woman of the Genessee", was captured by Indians when she was a child in Pennsylvania. She subsequently lived with the Indians of the Genessee Valley in New York state for seventy years, claiming that, "No people can live more happily than the Indians did in times of peace; their lives were a continual round of pleasures. Their wants were few and easily satisfied; and their cares were only for today. If peace ever dwelt with men, it was in former times, in the recesses from war." [3]

Strategy was as much a part of Indian warfare as it is in modern day battles, with the element of surprise being one of the primary objectives of any raiding party. "Surprise and strategem are as often employed by them as open force," claims one historian who witnessed those times first-hand. "Courage, art, and circumspection are the essential and indispensable qualifications of an Indian warrior. When war is once begun, each one strives to excel in displaying them, by stealing upon his enemy unawares, and deceiving and surprising him in various ways. On drawing near to an enemy's country, they endeavor as much as possible to conceal their tracks." [4]

Evidence of some of these early Indian battles has been found at various places in the state. Large quantities of war relics such as arrowheads and spearheads, as well as many skeletal remains, found at Duncan's Island near Harrisburg have led to the conclusions that a large battle was fought in that area. Similar sites have been found near Millerstown (Perry County), Tuscarora (Schuylkill County), and Standing Stone (Huntingdon County). The South Mountains, too, certainly saw their share of battles between Indians and whites during the French and Indian War when these hills were kind of a natural barrier between the settlers of Adams County and the Indians to the west. But even before that, the sound of the war whoop or the sight of warriors painted for war was not uncommon here. For it was through this very section that the Virginia Path, or Great Trail, wound its way toward Maryland and the Carolinas.

The Great Trail was the easternmost Iroquois war path used by the Cherokees and Catawbas on their raids into

Pennsylvania or by the Iroquois on their raids south. There were other warrior paths in Pennsylvania besides the Great Trail - all running north to south. Some of these, however, were not used by raiding parties, but were called warrior paths by the early settlers anyway, merely because they were not commonly used by white traders. So there were "warrior paths" in Huntingdon County, Greene County, and in Clearfield County. There was also the Great Warrior Path which followed the Susquehanna River. But the Virginia Path is the one that came closest to the Indian face in the South Mountains. The approximate route of this "true" warrior path through southern Pennsylvania was from Harrisburg, through Carlisle, to Shippensburg, and then to Chambersburg and south, which meant that the trail passed within ten miles of the stone face.

Perhaps the first South Mountain settlers, or some of their descendants, found the likeness on the rock, and, knowing about the location of the Great Trail and also about the many Indian warriors that once frequented this area, created the legend. They would, no doubt, have heard something of the Tuscarora Indians (a branch of the Iroquois) who lived in Franklin County at one time, and they might have known even a little about how the Indians conducted their raids. Such information may have been enough to prompt some creative individual to invent the story about the stone face. On the other hand, there is just as much reason to think that the legend could have come from the Indian tribes that lived in the area. Details in the legend do agree with the Indians' own descriptions of the way a raiding party conducted the business.

"Long time ago my tribe was at war with our enemy of the south-land, the Cherokees or "Oh-ya-dah", the cave-dweller, and often called the people of the Red", claimed one Iroquois story teller. "This happened when a war party was on its way to the land of the "Oh-ya-dah" to come back with as many scalps as it can. Now it seems in those times they had a head chief in command in every war party. It was his duty to give thanks every morning as they got up, before they ate their morning meal.

"It was the custom in those days to take their time in their march to the enemy country, to conserve their strength for the coming battle. So it took many days before they reached their destination. Every night, upon retiring, the head chief would cause warriors to stand guards at certain distance and there to give alarm in case of attack." [5]

At this point the Iroquois account departs from historical facts and enters a fantasy realm which many Indians once considered to be as real as the everyday world of sight and sound. In the land of Indian legends, strange things sometimes happened when a band of warriors was on the warpath - or at least to this one particular band, which had to seek shelter when a terrific storm blew in one night. As the storm heightened in intensity the band of warriors "noticed what seemed like sparks of fire flying with the wind." "All at once they saw a monster head with its long hair whirling in all directions. Now it seems this monster head was the power of this wind-storm, as the trees of the forest just snapped in two before this head reached the tree. One could see its trail as trees were leveled to the ground." [5]

The quaint story of the flying head certainly is entertaining to read, but it also makes it easy to think that if the Indians could have a legend about flying heads, they also could have a story about a derelict sentry's spirit being cast into a rock. In fact, this punishment of eternal vigilance would, no doubt, seem appropriate to them. The unfortunate guard that had failed so miserably in doing his job would have gotten, in the minds of his contemporaries, just the punishment he deserved. In fact, Indian braves might have once used this story to teach their young men about responsibility, showing them the stone face on the mountain as an example of what could happen when a warrior didn't do his duty.

Footnote on the Indian face: It appears that in recent years the rocks that formed the likeness of the original Indian face have broken away and slid down the mountain. The author has tried unsuccessfully on at least six separate occasions to find the sculpted face and the original, whose photo appeared in a Gettysburg newspaper eighty years ago. However, there is another natural formation that passes for the Indian face today.

The other natural formation that is now
pointed out as the Indian sentinel's face.
Michaux State Forest, Franklin County

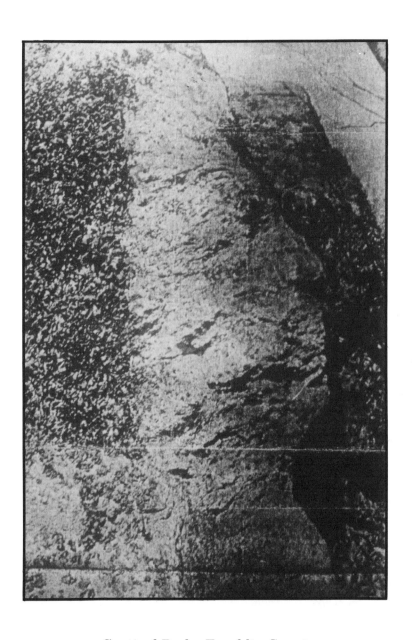

Sentinel Rock, Franklin County
(Photo of the original face which accompanied
the *Gettysburg Times* news article)

THE ENCHANTED BULLET HOLE

Descriptions of the battles that took place during the Civil War often include references to how intense the musket fire could be, and, consequently, how thick the concentration of flying musket balls would get. The battle at Gettysburg on July first through third, 1863, was not an exception to the rule. In fact, if anything, Gettysburg may have established some new standards for concentrated musket firing. At least there is one first-hand account that would seem to indicate that such a record was established. During the second day of the battle at Gettysburg, one soldier noticed that some of the slab fences along the Emmitsburg Road "were so completely perforated with bullet holes that you could scarcely place a half inch rule between them. One 1 1/4 inch thick board was indeed a curiosity. It was 16 feet long, 14 inches broad and was perforated with 836 musket balls." [1]

The Emmitsburg Road was not the only place that soldiers at Gettysburg must have experienced such a devastating hail of bullets. One of the relics on display in a museum at the National Battlefield Park is mute evidence of the deadly rain of fire that was often typical of the three day battle. Shown in a display case of the museum are two musket balls that were found on the blood-soaked fields after the terrible clash ended. The two minnie balls are fused together, apparently as a result of a mid-air collision.

There were, of course, soldiers in the midst of all these small messengers of death, and many men only survived because they had a large amount of luck. It almost seems that some men had the protection of a divine hand in order to have survived at all, and there's probably no better example of such fellows than "Snap" Rouser of Company K, First Pennsylvania Reserves, a unit that would later be described as "the boys who fought at home".[2] In fact, it was when they were fighting the Confederates around Little Round Top that "Snap" made the history books. Sometime, in the midst of this particular skirmish, Rouser had the misfortune to get hit with a Rebel's minnie ball. Normally a man would have been killed instantly if hit where Rouser got shot, but the young Federal was lucky. He is said to be the only known soldier in the entire Union army to have stopped a minnie ball with his front teeth. Rouser was lucky, all right, considering there were 51,000 men who lost their lives during the battle at Gettysburg.

He probably was always reminded of his amazing good fortune when he smiled, if he survived the rest of the war, because Rouser must have had his front teeth knocked out when they stopped the minnie ball that would have surely killed him otherwise. But Rouser wasn't the only "lucky" soldier in the war. There were others who escaped death by margins just as narrow as his, or even narrower. One-hundred years ago there were probably many veterans still alive who had experienced a close brush with death during the War Between the States, and each man might have considered his to be the closest. If so, then John Riter and Jacob Dunkle, both of Centre County, would have been top contenders for the honor.

John Riter settled near Centre Hall, Centre County, after serving with a company of sharpshooters from Massachusetts during the Civil War. In Centre County he became a respected veterinarian, but his biggest claim to fame was probably the tales he could tell of his wartime experiences, including the story of the battle where he lost his eye. At the Battle of Cold Harbor, June 30, 1864, Riter "was in the engagement where the lead flew thickest." [3] Cold Harbor was a battle that ended as a terrible defeat for Union troops, and it was a fight where Federals encountered Rebel musket fire so intense that "some Union lines collapsed one upon the other like toppling dominoes." [4]

Riter may have been one of those "dominoes", for he probably went down like a ton of bricks when a deadly greeting from the enemy lines, "entered the Doctor's left eye, and passed to a position back of the ear." [3] Riter survived his wound, but the bullet remained embedded in his brain, where it caused him "much pain" for the rest of his life. [3]

Not too far down the valley from Riter, in the little village of Aaronsburg, lived a fellow-soldier named Jacob Dunkle. Dunkle had been wounded in much the same way Riter had been, and perhaps the two men knew one another. If they were not acquainted before, then they surely must have spoken after Dunkle's coughing fit became a news item. It seems that one day, in 1894, Dunkle experienced "a severe coughing spell" [3] which was serious enough to call for the services of a doctor. During one particularly bad episode, the Aaronsburg soldier coughed up the bullet that had been imbedded in his brain all those years since the war. Jacob Dunkle survived this last wartime onslaught, but his unusual coughing fit must have impressed his doctor considerably, for it was later reported that "the bullet is now in possession of Dr. Frank of Millheim". [3]

Jacob Dunkle's bullet would have been an unusual relic of the Civil War, just as Snap Rouser's would have been if it had been saved, but there was also another bullet that was fired at Gettysburg, and its story is not one of hate, but one of love. Oftentimes in narratives of the Civil War descriptions of troop movements and battles dominate the text, and the human side of the war is forgotten. However, at Gettysburg there is one human interest story about the battle that has never failed to interest anyone that has heard it. Nonetheless, many people, unless they've visited the Gettysburg house where the incident occurred, have never known about the rest of the story and the legend which it spawned.

During the battle at Gettysburg many residents of the town remained in their homes because they felt certain that Confederate troops would never break through Union lines and enter Gettysburg itself. Two such residents were Georgia McClellan and her sister, Mary Virginia Wade. Georgia's husband, John Lewis McClellan, was a Union soldier who was away at war on June 26, 1863, when Georgia gave birth to their first son. It was the birth of Lewis Kenneth McClellan that prompted Mary Virginia, called "Jennie" by her friends and family, to move in with Georgia. Although Jennie must have known that the town was sandwiched between opposing armies, her desire to help her sister with the new baby and with household chores overcame any fears she might have had about the struggle that was being waged on the outskirts of the community.

During those long hours together in the McClellan house on Baltimore Street, Jennie and Georgia probably listened to the battle as it surged back and forth through places like the peach orchard, the wheatfield, the bloody angle, and the "slaughter pen" at Devil's Den. As they listened to the roar of the cannons and the firing of muskets, the womens' thoughts and conversation also probably turned to their own "soldier boys". Georgia's husband was many miles from home, and, for all she knew, was in the middle of a battle just like the one she was listening to at her own front door. Jennie's thoughts at this time were probably on her fiance "Jack", Corporal Johnston H. Skelly, who was with the boys in blue somewhere in Virginia.

Jack Skelly and Jennie Wade had been "sweethearts" since they were kids, and several months before

Jack had gone off to war he and Jennie had decided they would be married in September. Not too long after Skelly's departure he wrote Jennie a letter which reaffirmed his love for her and for his country. It was a letter which Jennie kept, but she would never get to tell her fiance how much it meant to her.

The first day of the Battle of Gettysburg, July first, had ended in the retreat of Union troops through the town. Union reinforcements arrived during the night, and by July second Union forces had established solid defenses on places like Seminary Ridge, Culp's Hill, and Little Round Top. When July second dawned, the little town of Gettysburg awoke to find that its eastern, northeastern, and southern sections were battlegrounds. There might have been some residents who, on July second, began to have some doubts about whether Gettysburg would be safe from southern invasion, but Jennie Wade and her sister must not have been among them. The two women went about their normal household routine, with Jennie baking bread in the kitchen.

It must have been the smell of the baking bread that led two Union soldiers passing by the McClellan house to stop and ask for food. Jennie gave them each some bread from the first batch she had made that day, and returned to the second batch, which she was mixing in a baking tray. Perhaps the presence of the Union soldiers made Jennie and Georgia feel too secure, too confident. Even a stray bullet that entered the parlor window a short time later didn't stop Jennie from baking her bread.

However, the young girl should have reflected upon the warning the bullet seemed to carry.

The stray missle did not fall harmlessly to the floor. Instead it whizzed into the parlor and hit Mrs McClellan's bedpost, falling down right next to her head. Mrs. McClellan's bed had been moved to the parlor from her upstairs bedroom in order that she might recover from her childbirth more readily, and as she lay there in the parlor that morning she must have been too frightened to go back to sleep after the bullet came through the window. If she was still awake, she then most certainly heard another bullet crash through the inner and outer doors at the back of her house.

It is thought that the bullet that entered the rear door of the McClellan house came from a Confederate sharpshooter who had been hiding in John Rupp's tannery across the street. The sharpshooter was most likely aiming at some Union soldiers, but his musket ball found another mark instead. The bullet that came through the house doors certainly would have made enough noise to frighten anyone, but Jennie probably didn't even have time enough to be startled. After cleanly passing through the doors, the bullet hit her in the back, passed on through her body, came out her neck, and landed in the baking tray. She was killed instantly; an untimely end for a young lady whose life was filled with such promise. However, Jenny's Wade's death became the basis for a legend that, in some peoples' minds, offers hope to others much like herself.

There was also another native of Gettysburg whose fate would be determined by the battle there, and whose death would become inextricably entwined with that of Jennie Wade's. Although his demise is filled with as much pathos and irony as that of Jennie's, this young soldier's story is not as widely heralded. Nonetheless, Wesley Culp's tale must be told if the Jennie Wade legend is to be understood

Wesley Culp grew up in Gettysburg, where his family had lived for several generations. His grandfather's farm was here, and Culp had often played there as a boy. But Wes Culp was not one who was swayed by familial bonds. Several years before the outbreak of the war, he left the place of his birth and migrated to what is now Shepherdstown, West Virginia. At that time the peaceful little country hamlet was in Virginia, but five years later, during the height of the Civil War, the western inhabitants of Virginia determined that the bonds of statehood were weaker than the their northern sympathies, and so they seceded from their home state to form the state of West Virginia. However, by that time, Wesley Culp was already committed to the southern cause, and was clad in the grey uniform of a Rebel soldier.

Shortly after he had arrived in Shepherdstown, Culp's interests were attracted to a local militia unit that seemed to be a glamorous outlet for a young man's energies. War clouds were not yet gathering on the horizon, and the main business of the home guards appeared to be providing young men a place to socialize and a way to impress the local girls by marching around in dashing uniforms. Appealing incentives like this were probably the main reason that Wesley signed up with the guards, and he most likely enjoyed the camaraderie for a while. However, the young troopers turned serious one day when the call to war finally came, and the soldiers, to a man, joined the Confederate Army.

Oblivious to the horrors of real war, Wesley Culp's guard unit was placed in a Virginia regiment that would, after the first Battle of Bull Run, become known as the "Stonewall" brigade because of their spirited and successful defense in the face of overwhelming enemy troops. It was a name they took with them to Gettysburg two years later.

Their march toward Pennsylvania was not uneventful. Near Winchester, Virginia, they encountered Federal forces, and a small engagement ensued. Ironically enough, the boys in blue were troops that had been recruited in Gettysburg, and among them was a man who had been one of Wes Culp's best boyhood chums. After the battle was over, Culp somehow learned that his friend had been wounded, and he managed to find him among the casualties. The wounded corporal's main concern was that his sweetheart in Gettysburg be told of his whereabouts, and Culp agreed that if he ever got back to that place he would deliver the message to the girl, whose name was Jennie Wade. Later that night, when Jack Skelly died of his wounds on that Virginia battlefield, he probably expired thinking that at least his betrothed would know that his last thoughts were of her.

When the Stonewall Brigade did finally reach Gettysburg the landscape that spread out before them must have been familiar to Wes Culp. Scenes of his boyhood probably came flooding into his mind as his brigade marched past familiar farms and fields, but he was still surely surprised when they were ordered to dig in on an elevation that was once part of his grandfather's farm. It was the same hill he had romped upon as a boy, perhaps making pretend charges here when he played army with his friends. The irony of the situation could not have escaped him when he realized that he was about to fight a real battle near the little knoll which still bore his family's name.

Any visions of boyhood pleasures that Wes Culp had on Culp's Hill that day must have been short-lived. The reality of the moment would have crowded out any pleasurable thoughts, prompting this dedicated young soldier to remember his promise to Jack Skelly. One tale says that Culp actually sent a message to Jennie Wade's mother, asking her to meet him the next day. It was a meeting that was not to be. On July second, Wesley Culp paid the supreme sacrifice. He died on Culp's Hill, defending the place where he had once experienced the joys of childhood.

"So the message he had for this woman didn't matter," explained the former park ranger who was an expert on the human interest stories of the conflict at Gettysburg. "Because the woman that was Skelly's fiancee was Jennie Wade, and Jennie Wade was the only civilian killed in the battle. And when they carried the body through the house to the other side of the house, a photograph, a little daguerreotype, of Skelly fell out of her pocket. We're really not sure, she didn't have a ring or anything like that - whatever they did back in those days - but maybe the only people that knew she was engaged would have been Culp, Skelly, and Jennie. Nevertheless, it's kind of an odd coincidence. All three died without knowing the others fate." [5]

Visitors that come to the Gettysburg battlefield today often visit the former McClellan home on Baltimore Street. Here they are shown throughout the structure, which still looks almost like it did on that fateful day in 1863. The kitchen where Jennie was baking her bread has been authentically reproduced, right down to the baking tray. Upstairs, Jennie's picture is hanging on the wall of one of the bedrooms, and it silently expresses the innocence and sweetness that must have been a dominant part of her personality. However, the one major piece of the house that has been carefully protected throughout the years and which most eloquently bears silent witness to the sad thing that happened that July day in 1863 is the outside door with the bullet hole. It is this bullet hole which is the foundation for the legend that clings to the house on Baltimore Street.

If someone didn't know the legend, they would wonder why the bullet hole is now smoothly polished all around and much larger in size than it must have been originally. The explanation for the bullet hole's condition today rests with the legend, which states that if an unmarried girl inserts her finger into the hole she will, within a year's time, receive a marriage proposal. No explanations as to the origin of this quaint belief seem to exist, but it is not hard to guess that someone that knew the saga of Jennie's unfulfilled love, and perhaps knew Jennie herself, created the myth. On the other hand, the legend may just have been invented by a savvy owner in order to attract paying tourists. In any case, the fable of the bullet hole does seem to be based on Jennie's tragic love story, and there are some who put much faith in the legend's claims.

At least one young lady once felt that the legend had special significance in her life, assuming that the following letter on display in the house is genuine. Since the missive is dated July 4, 1976 there were probably many other young ladies over the years who were just as convinced as the writer of the following epistle that their matrimonial successes were aided by the powers of the bullet hole:

Sir; I must tell you my story. You have told the superstition about the bullet hole in the door many times. And all young ladies would declare they are not superstitious. So, of course, neither am I. But half in fun and whole earnest the particular finger is usually thrust into the hole. I have an awfully good excuse. It was at Easter time we brought our Girl Scouts to your house on our way to Washington. And since the spell doesn't work on girls under twenty-one, I put my finger in to please them.

That sounds reasonable, doesn't it ? Secretly I hoped, but sincerely felt that it wouldn't possibly happen. Now you have probably guessed the result - if you wish to call it that. In May he drove 650 miles to see me (I had never expected to see him again). We decided we were deeply in love. He proposed. My diamond ring is to come this week - for my birthday. And the wedding will be no later than the next spring. I assure you the story is true in every detail. I still won't admit I am superstitious, but perhaps you are more definitely justified in leading others' faith to hope. May others find similar happiness.

Sincerely, Alma [6]

Although Jennie Wade's life ended tragically and she never had the opportunity to fulfill her destiny with the man that she loved, she nonetheless might be satisfied with what has been done with her story. She would, no doubt, be happy to know that her sad tale is the basis for a legend that now seems to be a source of hope to young girls much like herself.

Jennie Wade and the Enchanted Bullet Hole

150

FIDDLING PHANTOMS

People up in Indiana County's Mahoning Valley still remember the house of the fiddling ghost. Although the odd-looking structure burned down under mysterious circumstances about forty years ago, the place is still recalled when folks in Smicksburg talk about "spooks" and other things that are apt to send chills up a person's spine. The old residence was always considered different due to its unusual architecture, but, according to legend, it wasn't until a murder occurred there, around the time that the tracks were being laid for the Rochester and Pittsburgh Railroad, that the house really became a popular object of curiosity.

The railroad, which was later to become part of the Baltimore and Ohio rail system, would open up an area that had been isolated for centuries. In fact, northern Indiana County was, at that same time, still referred to as the territory "up above the purchase". [1] This curious phrase originated back in 1768 when the Penns bought (many would say cheated away) from the Indians that part of northern Pennsylvania that lies above a line running from Cherry Tree, Indiana County, to Kittanning, Armstrong County. That purchase was the last that the Penns made from the Indians, and so the lands north of the "purchase line" were among the last in the state to be fully settled. Once as common a phrase

151

in Indiana County as the "Mason and Dixon Line" is to those in southern Pennsylvania, the term "Purchase Line" is preserved today in the name of an Indiana County town that lies on the original purchase boundary.

About twenty miles above the Indian purchase line, and close to where Mahoning Creek intersects the Baltimore and Ohio tracks, there is a township road near the town of Smicksburg, that is called Rossmoyne Road. The highway has only been paved within the last couple decades, and so the area was not well-traveled for some time. However, there may just have been another reason for the lack of traffic through here over the years, and that reason might be because not too far off of Rossmoyne, along a dusty country road, once sat the house of the fiddling ghost. There is just a vacant lot there now, the charred remains of the old house bull-dozed away by edict of the township authorities. Nonetheless, the story of the place still lives on in the memory of those who know the legend, and perhaps the notes from the ghostly fiddler can still be heard as well if passersby listen closely. However, the possibility of hearing the music probably depends on whether one believes in such things or not. On the other hand, it is interesting to note that this legend is similar to that of another, more famous, fiddling ghost in the state. It also has its counterparts in Europe, where ghostly musicians have entertained people for centuries.

The Mahoning Valley legend of the fiddling ghost begins at the time when two men, apparently not related, came to the valley to help lay the Rochester and Pittsburgh Railroad tracks. The men lived in a house near Smicksburg, which they either bought or rented. Their residence was considered odd-looking for that day, but, in fact, it was probably a bit ahead of its times because it was more like what we would call an "A-frame" now. However, despite any "modern" appearances the place might have exhibited, there was a decidedly old-time aspect to one of its inhabitants.

According to the legend, one of the men living in the house was in some ways a bit of a throwback to an earlier period. It is said that he was.an old-time fiddler who was so adept that he was often asked to play at barn dances and other social events. The old tale doesn't state whether or not the fiddler liked to boast about his skills, but if he was as good as the legend states, then he might have at least been forgiven if he made a statement like legendary old-time country fiddler "Uncle" Dave Macon once made. "I can fiddle 'taters' off the vine," was "Uncle" Dave's personal claim to fame, and no doubt the Mahoning Valley fiddler would have been a regular at any playing contests held in the area if he was anywhere as good as "Uncle" Dave. However, anyone that good did not get, and stay, that way without lots of practice. It takes hours and hours of practice, day in and day out, to become a great fiddler, and that is probably why the old Mahoning Valley legend claims such practicing may have led to a murder.

Perhaps the incessant sound of a fiddle gradually grated upon the nerves of the other resident of the odd-looking house. The second man may not have appreciated fine old fiddle tunes as much as his companion, and the constant music may have been too much. After hearing repeated renditions of tunes like "The Lop-eared Mule", "Over the Stump and Back Again", or others similar to these collected by Samuel Bayard in Greene County in the 1940's [2], the non-fiddler may have snapped. At least the legend considers him to be a prime suspect in the death of his friend. According to the story, one day neither man showed up for work at the railroad. Later on that day, when people came to their house to look for the men, they found the fiddler stabbed to death, his fiddle broken to bits, and his bow snapped in half. The second man was never seen again.

Eventually the sensational occurrence became less of a topic in the valley, but rumors about the house persisted. Tales began to surface about people who saw strange things as they passed by the deserted place on nights of a full moon when there was a nip in the air and frost on the ground. On such nights there seemed to be, so said the tales, a ghostly white vapor clinging to the peak of the house's steep roof. If observed long enough, so went other accounts, the vapor took the form of the murdered fiddler, who could be seen sitting up there playing his instrument.

Those who were brave enough to stay and watch claimed that they could even hear the fiddler's music sometimes. [1]

Today the house of the fiddling ghost is gone, and those who know the legend are disappearing as well. However, there may be others who read this story and decide, on some frosty night when the moon is full, to visit the vacant lot where the house of the fiddling ghost once stood. They will, no doubt, hope to see the ghost, or at least hear the strains of some old fiddle tune like "Hell's Broke Loose in Smicksburg". However, before they go to the trouble, they should read on and learn about the tale of another fiddling ghost.

Anyone who has heard of Ole Bull State Park in Potter County has probably wondered just who was this man for whom the park is named. Ole Bull would probably be saddened by this lack of fame, for in his day he was an international celebrity. Bull was born in Norway in 1810, eventually becoming a violin virtuoso whose concert tours throughout Europe, Canada, the West Indies, and the United States were greeted with enthusiasm. Even the great violinist Paganini was impressed with Ole Borneman Bull's technique, and the Norwegian's fame preceded him when he returned to the United States in 1852 for another concert tour.

Ole Bull had another reason for returning to this country in 1852, and that was because he wanted to look for land here to "found a new Norway, consecrated to liberty, baptized with independence, and protected by the Union's mighty flag".[3] Discouraged by Sweden's subjugation of his native country, as dictated by a settlement made at the Congress of Vienna in 1815, the patriotic young musician wanted to create a place of freedom for fellow countrymen who were as disillusioned as he was with the constraints placed upon them by the aristocracy.

The idealistic young Norwegian was eventually introduced to John F. Cowan of Williamsport, who "sold" Bull 11,000 acres of land along Kettle Creek in Pennsylvania's "Black Forest" country. The territory and climate reminded Bull of his native Norway, and he began to build his colony in earnest. Eventually a great stone castle "of feudal proportions" [4] was built for the great master's residence, and the towns of New Norway, New Bergen, Oleona, and Walhalla were planned. Norwegian settlers attacked the wilderness that was Ole Bull's "Promised Land" with a vengeance, but the land was never meant for farming, and the progress was slow. The number of settlers peaked at 800 in 1853, and then the bad news came that Bull had been cheated. The lands that Cowan had sold him were not lands that Cowan owned, which was not surprising to those who knew the speculator as someone of dubious honesty. Said one man, [I] 'would as soon pick the bait out of a steel trap as to have any dealings with him!" [5]

Ole Bull's colony fell apart after Cowan's land scheme came to light. The great castle overlooking Kettle Creek was never completed, and the State Department of Forestry eventually dismantled the massive stone walls that had been erected. Today only the town of Oleona still lives on to commemorate the ambitious dreams of the young violinist who inspired so many with his music. Descriptions of that music have come down to us over the years, and they preserve a flavor of just how inspiring the violinist must have been when he got out his Stradivarius and began to play.

"It was the finest music I ever heard," recalled W. H. Sanderson, who heard Bull play at the Jersey Shore High School in 1852. [6] A similar testimony came down from Warren Wycoff, noted guide and big game hunter of the Cross Fork area of Potter County during the 1920' and 30's. Wycoff's father had heard Bull play, and the master's music reached the heart of even this rough-hewn backwoodsman. "Bull's music made you see the scenes the music was written about," was the way the old mountaineer would later describe the notes he had heard.[7] It was a surprising comment coming from someone not usually prone to such emotional thoughts, but Bull's music apparently had similar effects on many folks. There were others who heard the master play, and claimed he could "reproduce the rush and roar of rapid streams, the frolic of the winds through the rocky glens, and the tempest's crash on the mountain top." [8]

157

Despite his great talent and his many critically acclaimed successes in the concert halls of the world, Ole Bull was emotionally and financially ruined by his misdealings with John Cowan. It is said that when he realized his dreams had been shattered, "the prince of violinists" went mad, "wandering off into the mountains half-crazy with grief, playing his violin far into the night." Then, before recovering his composure and returning to his beloved castle, "he broke the instrument and buried it in the hillside." [9]

The Ole Bull legend has grown over the years, and, as common with many such tales, has even taken on some supernatural aspects. Today, so states the current version of the legend, campers and hikers who find themselves near the site of the violinist's castle will, on certain days of the year, "hear Ole Bull playing Beethoven's Eighth Sonata as the wind whistles through the trees". [10]

Although there may be those who think they may have heard the strains of Ole Bull's violin in the state park that now bears his name, there are other places where ghostly music has been heard as well. Indiana County's Mahoning Valley is, of course, one such place, but there are many castles in Europe where similar tales once abounded.

One of the most famous haunted castles in Great Britain is Cortachy Castle, the ancestral home of the Earls of Airlie. Here it was once believed that the sound of a ghostly drummer often foretold "the speedy death of a member of the Ogilvie family".[11] Legend has it that the ghost is that of a drummer who had incurred the wrath of a previous Lord Airlie. The drummer's infraction was apparently a serious one, for the legend goes on to state that he was stuffed into his own drum and thrown out of one of the castle's tower windows. It is the vengeful ghost of this murdered drummer, so says the legend, that reminds the Ogilvies of the black mark in their history whenever one of them is about to die.

There are certainly many other examples of musical ghosts in the British Isles, the "harper" of Inveraray Castle being another fine example, and so the story line is an old one. Nonetheless it is a fascinating one for those who enjoy the odd and the mysterious. It is indeed fun to speculate on the possibility of such things actually happening, but those of a less romantic mindset probably prefer to look at these things in the same light as the gentleman from Smicksburg who, when I asked him about the fiddling ghost, and ghosts in general, replied, "They're about all died off. The new generation don't keep up with them. You see, now they have television. They have all that horror stuff on [there] instead of telling these good stories around the table in the evening". [12]

Site of Ole Bull's Partially Erected Castle
Near Oleona, Potter County

The historical marker reads:
At this spot in 1852 Ole Bull, world renowned violinist who arrived with 800 Norwegian colonists that year, commenced the erection of a stone castle; but the failure of the colonization project due to faulty land titles led to the abandonment of the castle; and the colony the year following.

Picture courtesy of Penna. State Archives, Public Relations Office Photo file # 5014, RG-6 Dept. of Forests and Waters

NIGHT SCREAMS

Chickies Rock County Park in Lancaster County has gained a reputation over the decades as one of the most haunted sections in the entire state. It seems that every year a new ghost story or another episode of the supernatural is told about this scenic region which overlooks the Susquehanna River and the Hellam Hills near the town of Columbia. Several interesting collections of these tales have been published in recent years, those by local author Dorothy Fiedel being among the most complete. However, despite her diligent efforts, Fiedel still hasn't managed to preserve all the singular stories of the region, including the curious tale of the haunted railroad tunnel. Perhaps the reason for that is because the story is a perfect example of how someone takes some real history and uses it to explain what to them appears to be supernatural events. At least that's what the descendants of Michael Keppler are convinced has happened. Some of the rangers at Chickies Park, on the other hand, are convinced that Keppler's untimely end offers a perfect explanation for the uncanny events now occurring where he died in the waning years of the nineteenth century.

Michael Keppler's mangled remains were discovered in the old railroad tunnel that once served as a portal for the train that carried materials to and from the large iron furnaces located nearby. Legend and history differ markedly on how Keppler ended up in that tunnel just outside the iron manufactory, and so this part of the legend remains shrouded in mystery. However, the Henry Clay Iron Works was once a real place, and there's no doubt about that. Situated along the Susquehanna between the river towns of Marietta and Columbia, the Clay Works was once a major employer in this part of Lancaster County. No definite explanation for the facility's name seems to have come down to the present day, but the owner must have been an admirer of United States congressman Henry Clay, one of the most highly respected politicians in the United States during the years immediately preceding the Civil War.

Despite the fame of the person for whom it was named, most people today don't seem to realize that such a place as the Henry Clay Furnace even existed here along the scenic Susquehanna. There are few traces left of the original plant, and even though the old railroad bed that the rail tracks were laid upon can still be seen, the steel rails that once led to the furnace have been gone for years. However, there are other tracks, those of the Conrail system, that still lie along the river here, stretching under Route 30 and passing by the old rail yards in Columbia. Looking in the opposite direction, to the north toward Chickies Rock and Marietta, the keen observer will also see remains of a furnace – part of the original Henry Clay complex. Those who pause a little longer to look up river toward the impressive ledge known as Chickies Rock may also notice the dark and mysterious entrance to a tunnel that was painstakingly carved out of the solid rock face of Chickies Ridge. It is this same tunnel that serves as the setting for the chilling events that are preserved in the legend of this place. It is a legend, so say some of the local rangers, that begins with an architect who was educated at Heidelberg University, in the ancient West German city of Heidelberg.

According to the legend as it's told today, the architect, whose name was Michael Keppler, decided to immigrate to this country sometime in the late 1800's. Keppler, it is said, brought his wife and children along with him in order to find a better life, but that dream never came true. The legend claims there was no employment for architects in the section of Pennsylvania where Keppler settled, especially architectural jobs for those as highly educated as the young German. Therefore, in order to support his family, Keppler had to take a menial spot as a laborer in the Henry Clay Iron Works along the Susquehanna. Working close to a hot and dirty iron furnace every day, seven days a week for twelve hours a day, was an insult to someone educated in a prestigious seat of learning like Heidelberg, and Keppler's disposition supposedly changed from positive and genial to negative and argumentative.

The legend goes on to say that Michael Keppler became more and more irascible as time wore on, and he eventually tried to drown his desperation in bouts of prolonged drinking. Alcohol only made matters worse, and soon Keppler had no friends. Then his wife could take no more, and she kicked him out of the house. Keppler had no choice but to move into the company houses at the iron works and to live in cramped quarters with the other ironworkers. This proved to be the "last straw" and the once-genial architect was now apt to get angry over even smaller things than before. Even his drinking became more intense, and so, on the rare nights off from the fiery pits where he made his living, he could often be seen, sometimes with a bottle in his hand, staggering off to one of the many "watering holes" in Columbia. It was this combination of anger and liquor that ultimately led to his undoing, for Keppler was apt to erupt at the slightest provocation and so was often one of the combatants in any fights that erupted in the bars in Columbia.

These are the background details presented in the legend that is told about Michael Keppler today. They set the stage for the next part of the account that goes on to describe how Keppler met his untimely end. According to this segment, one night when Keppler was staggering off to one of his favorite drinking spots, he passed by the night watchmen who stood guard at the gates to the iron complex. They pleasantly bid him a good night, but he did not answer in kind, cursing at them instead. Later, in the "wee small hours" of the morning, these same watchmen saw Keppler returning, but not on foot. Instead, he was driving a horse and buggy, which presented a bit of a mystery to the men. It was a fancy outfit, one that was too expensive for anyone of Keppler's means. However, Keppler ignored their stares, and, despite their warnings, drove right into the railroad tunnel. Within minutes, the watchmen heard the train whistle, and then the "screams and shrieks of a man being shredded underneath the locomotive." [1]

The legend, as it's told now, does not end with Keppler's death. Instead, the account goes on to speculate about how this man of decidedly modest means ended up with a fancy horse and buggy. Did he steal it, and, in a drunken state, mistakenly drive into the tunnel, or did something more sinister happen? Perhaps someone forced him to drive the buggy into the tunnel where they could rob and murder him, and then lay his body on the tracks so the train would run over him. This would have been a good way to confuse those who later tried to ascertain cause of death. Whatever the case, the legendary accounts say that Keppler's spirit is a restless one due to his untimely and violent end. It is Keppler's spirit that haunts the place, or so say some of those who have had otherworldly experiences in the old Clay Works tunnel.

"Misfortune is often bestowed upon people that travel through that tunnel," claims one park ranger who has experienced some weird events there himself. "I don't know that I believe in all these things, but I did have a few experiences. Twice in one week my jeep got a flat tire when I was driving through that tunnel. Other than being a little bit upset at having to sit in the train yard changing tires while eight or ten Conrail workers kind of looked at me and laughed, I didn't think a whole lot of it. But then, a week later, almost to the hour, I got a flat tire in the exact same tire driving through that tunnel. I just assumed there was something in the bottom of this big puddle that forms there in the tunnel in the spring that was causing my tires to go flat." [1]

After a prolonged dry spell, the water in the tunnel dried up, thereby allowing a closer look. "I must've spent twenty or thirty minutes combing the bottom of that tunnel looking for anything I might've driven over that would give me a flat tire," explained the ranger. "I didn't find it." [1]

The mystery of the flat tires might have ended there, but something else occurred that seemed even more eerie. "The very last thing happened just a few weeks ago," continued the young man. "At that point I did not know this story [about Michael Keppler]. I was going through the tunnel about 9:30 PM and I thought I heard voices, and I'm not one who usually takes to hearing voices! I thought there was a reasonable explanation to this. I walked to the other end of the tunnel, and I just assumed people were walking on the property above me. But it was odd. I heard a man's voice, and he was talking, but nobody was answering him. I couldn't locate this voice, [and] I didn't find any cars parked down there. I haven't been real anxious to go back looking either! I'm not ready yet to say it was the spirit of Mr.

Keppler, but if I don't find something soon, I might start to become a believer!" [1]

Although there may be logical explanations for the young ranger's strange experience in the tunnel at Chickies Ridge, these types of peculiar events are perfect raw materials for the factories of the legendary world. The result of combining these ingredients with the story of Michael Keppler's murder results in the perfect ghost story. Nonetheless, the nagging questions and doubts still remain. Was there such a man as Michael Keppler, and, if so, are some of the man's biographical details preserved in the legend about the tunnel? It turns out that the answer to both questions is yes.

If Michael Keppler's spirit is a restless one, it may be because of the circumstances surrounding his unexplained death, which still leaves his descendants dissatisfied. On the other hand, he may be restless because of the way legend has sullied his name as a drunk and a thief. This second possibility doesn't rest well with his descendants either, and they are anxious to set the record straight.

Michael Keppler was a real person. Born in Bavaria in 1838, he was educated as an architect at Heidelberg University, just as the legend states. He immigrated to this country just prior to the Civil War, finding some employment here as an architect and builder. However, the work was sporadic and he did other types of things to supplement his income. "He was known as 'the old house mover', explained Keppler's great great grand daughter. "He used to move structures with block and tackle and mules. He developed all the equipment himself to do this."

"As far as the drinking goes, he was a typical German. They were hard-working and hard-drinking people. They all drank - the majority of them. There wasn't such a word as alcoholism, and so he liked his booze."

However, people apparently liked Keppler too. "The obituary in the paper said that he was a nice fella, and well liked by everyone," continued the family historian. "Apparently he was highly thought of, and maybe he was looked at with a little bit of awe because he did have an education. In those days very few people ever got out of eighth grade if they did go to school at all! But he wasn't a vagrant. He took care of his family, but, you know, not everybody's marriage is happy, and a lot of times it is the alcohol that drives the wedge."

"He never divorced. He and his wife had nine children, but he and she lived apart. He supported the family and he fixed things around the house. At the time of his death he was working in at the Clay Furnace. Exactly what he was doing, I don't know, but he lived in the tenant house, because things apparently at home weren't all 'hunky-dory'. So it's not a happy story, but it's a human story.

"Well, apparently, according to the newspaper, he had borrowed, *borrowed,* not *stolen*, he had borrowed somebody's wagon and team of horses and he went in town to have himself a few beers at a local pub. There were watchmen at the gate that led back to the Clay Furnace, and they saw him go out and talked to him. Everybody knew him, and they saw him come back, and they said 'Hey, you'd better be careful. You've had a little bit too much to drink!'

"Well, whatever, he went on down the tracks, and they didn't hear anything from him, and then they found out he had been hit by a train. They didn't find the wagon or the horses, and they had an inquest into his death, They assumed he had fallen off the wagon and had gotten run over by a train, but they didn't find any money in his pockets, and he always had money!

The suspicion that Michael Keppler had been robbed and then murdered on that sultry evening of July 12, 1893, plagued his children until they died. His grand daughter always stated that "momma and poppa always thought that maybe he was murdered", and his great great grand daughter agrees. "Hey, maybe this guy was robbed and killed," she speculates. "Somebody might have hit him over the head!" [2]

Michael Keppler was "buried in pieces" [2] in the Mount Bethel Cemetery in Columbia. However, some years later, when declining upkeep gave this "city of the dead" a decidedly "run down" look, his descendants had his remains exhumed and re-interred in Laurel Hill Memorial Park, near the Columbia High School. Although legendary lore states that a restless spirit is sometimes created when its body is reburied in ground that is not pleasing to the dead person, it can only be hoped that this has not disturbed poor Michael Keppler. He seems to have had enough trouble when he was alive, and now he should be allowed a peaceful existence while in the next world. Perhaps this small account will at least set the record straight somewhat. However, there still is the matter of the flat tires that seem to occur from time to time in that deserted area along the river.

Sometimes following one of those days in July and August we call "dog days", a warmer than usual night wind blows down from the Hellam Hills and across the cool waters of the nearby Susquehanna causing dense mists to rise off the river's surface. The thicker the mists, the more surreal the area becomes, especially when the fog forms a deathly white shroud over the Conrail tracks and seeps into the deserted railroad tunnel that once glowed with the coals of the steam engines traveling to and from the Henry Clay Furnace. The atmosphere seems unreal at such times, and perhaps that's why the odd tales persist. The ranger whose tires went flat, for example, may be glad to know that he's not alone in having such troubles.

In one of her several books on the uncanny tales of the area, Dorothy Fiedel tells the story of two couples who decided to have a picnic at Chickies Park in July of 1995. The young people decided to have their outing after dark, just so they could look for ghosts. However, the picnickers found out that it's really more fun to read about such things than to actually experience them first hand.

The details of that evening are recounted in Fiedel's book, but unexplainable flat tires were among the hair-raising events of the night. When the couples discovered the first flat, they replaced it with the spare tire. However, after they had cooked their supper (which was also fraught with problems) and eaten, they discovered that the spare was now flat too. Flat tires can be attributed to many normal causes, but in this case, after the tires went flat, there were, according to those who were there at the time, accompanying events that were decidedly abnormal. Probably the most frightening occurrences that night were the screams that suddenly emanated from the woods nearby, and then the ball of mist that formed on the hillside and began rolling toward the picnickers. As if that were not enough to send chills up the stiffest spine, the frightened couples then noticed that the air temperature dropped considerably and the nearby trees began swaying as though being swept by a violent blast of wind, even though the air was calm.

It could, of course, be argued that the picnickers let their imaginations "get the best of them" that July night in 1995. Mists do roll off the river on such nights, and flat tires do happen at odd times and places to everyone, oftentimes caused by normal objects that can not be identified. However, as far as the flat tires at Chickies Rock and the uncanny events that seem to accompany them, most people, I think, will decide not to investigate firsthand. Most folks probably feel the same way as the ranger who wasn't "real anxious to go back looking", or like one of the picnickers who says, "Don't be at Chickies Rock after dark!" [3]

The haunted railroad tunnel
Chickies Rock County Park,
Lancaster County

View of the city of Heidelberg, beside the Neckar River, and
Heidelberg University, West Germany
(Taken from the walls of Heidelberg Castle by the author,
September, 1998)

HAND TO HORN COMBAT

According to many old hunters who passed their stories on to me and whose lives stretched back into the latter part of the nineteenth century, there were a number of years during that period when the white-tailed deer was a rarity in Pennsylvania. Sometime around the turn of the century the white tails were so scarce that, claimed one old veteran of the chase, "you couldn't even see a doe or a buck!" [1] In fact, in some sections of the state this condition lasted until at least 1910 or later, a situation that often caused hunters to get excited when even the slightest signs of a deer were found. It is said that in those years prior to the 1920's, a deer hoofprint was an object of curiosity in many parts of Pennsylvania. "Children would walk miles to see a deer track" claimed one person, and such imprints would inspire hunters to get out their best tracking hounds in hopes of bagging a big buck.[2] With the advent of the Roaring Twenties, however, the white-tailed deer became a more common sight in Pennsylvania.

Some said the turn-around was due to extensive lumbering operations that had begun in Virginia, the theory being that the deer were driven northward because of the destruction of their habitat to the south. Although this suggestion could explain some of the increase in the deer population in Pennsylvania around that time, it may have been an idea based more on denial than on fact. There is, indeed, another possible explanation for the

175

rebirth of the deer herd in Pennsylvania around the turn of the century, and it has to do more with a decrease in hunting excesses rather than with the greed of the lumber kings.

Prior to 1900 there were no game laws in Pennsylvania, and for some time after the laws were passed many veteran hunters chose to ignore them. The new restrictions took some getting used to, and even those who enforced them occasionally appeared to "look the other way". At least that was the perception of many of the law-abiding hunters, who claimed that the wardens "wouldn't prosecute unless they had to." [1]. The honest hunters knew who the outlaws were, and some felt that the game wardens had to know too. However, the reason officials chose to overlook the violators was not a mystery in the minds of the locals who subscribed to a "relative" explanation for the lack of action on the part of the wardens.

Family ties were quite extensive in the sparsely-populated rural areas of that day, and the fact that "everyone was related in some way" [1] made it likely that a hunting rogue and a game warden were at least distant cousins. Although it was his duty to arrest anyone who broke a game law, a warden may have indeed decided on occasion that it would be far wiser not to do so than to incur the wrath of mutual friends and close-knit relatives. On the other hand, it wouldn't have taken too many game offenders to make a noticeable difference, and so overkill was probably at least a contributing factor that kept the deer population here at minimal levels until the game laws began to be enforced more strictly. However, in some cases the deer did manage, or at least appeared to try, to fight back - to even the score with their executioners.

Old-time deer hunter Jackson Stover, who lived in the tiny mountain village of Coburn, near the confluence of Elk and Penns Creeks in Centre County, had the misfortune to shoot one such deer sometime during the first two decades of the twentieth century. Stover was a an avid devotee of the chase, and so he developed the skills and knowledge any good Nimrod needs to insure that he gets his buck every year. One proven technique the old hunter used for increasing his chances of seeing that nice big eight or ten "point" was to keep a block of salt, or "salt lick", set up in the foot hills below Paddy Mountain in Penn Township. Deer were attracted to this rare treat, and Stover often laid in wait nearby so he could "pot" the biggest bucks as they stood savoring the saline taste of the salt blocks. And if there happened to be more than one "trophy" buck wander in to the salt lick in any given year, Stover would shoot them all. Like many of the old hunters who had hunted in the days before game laws were introduced, Stover's hunting ethics were still rooted in the past, and so he was not hesitant about shooting does or bucks any time of the year, whether it was deer season or not.

The old Nimrod must have had quite a collection of magnificent antlers displayed in his house, the result of his many years of harvesting deer whenever they crossed his path, but there was one set of horns that were not part of his collection. This missing set may have even diminished the pleasure he got from admiring all the others that hung in profusion on his walls, for the missing antlers would have been from the buck that got away: the one that fought back.

The story of Stover's fighting stag began one day when the cagey hunter was "treed" near his salt lick. He had climbed up to a deer stand fastened in a tree above the lick, and he sat there silently, perhaps contemplating his chances of bringing down a buck with the biggest antlers anyone had ever seen. It wasn't long before a large buck did wander into the clearing below. Although probably not nearly as big as the one that Stover may have been hoping for, he shot it anyway, and, thinking he had killed it, came down out of the tree to "dress" the animal.

As Stover began the bloody work of "gutting" the fallen buck, it suddenly revived. After fully recovering its senses, the wounded stag stood up, and immediately after that its natural survival instincts took over. Much to the hunter's surprise, the "dead" deer became an enraged blur of horns and hide which began chasing him around the tree where the deer-stand was located. The buck managed to gore the frightened hunter in the legs with its horns several times, but fortunately Stover had a little dog along with him, and it finally started to bark in a high pitched frenzy. Despite its puny size, the little cur's yips unnerved the buck, and the noise scared the deer away. Too surprised and exhausted to pursue his "dead" buck, Stover decided to call it a day, and he never caught the stag; but it is told that he "carried the scars of that deer's horns for the rest of his life". [3]

There was another Centre County hunter whose fight with a buck was even more desperate than Jackson Stovers. In this case, the hunter had his dog along with him too, which once again proved to be a stroke of luck. John Lingle's encounter occurred over the mountains lying to the south of Coburn during a time described as "years ago [when] the deer weren't very plentiful". [4]

"Now I heard John Lingle, he was an old man, tell that they were out hunting, and they only had these muzzle-loaders that fired one shot," began the former resident of Poe Valley. The nearby lumbering town of Poe Paddy is now only a memory, but every year the wondrously wild Poe Valley State Park that has been sensibly preserved by the Commonwealth, along with surrounding state forest land, attracts hundreds of visitors seeking its solitude and its natural charms. Few are aware of the interesting stories that could once be heard about this region, including the story of John Lingle's fight with a deer.

"Well, they were in Poe Valley, and they chased these deer from Little Poe Mountain down to Big Poe Mountain," continued the valley native who once knew John Lingle personally. "Now this is true. They heard shots, [but] they didn't know right which way. Then pretty soon he heard a dog barking. This was, now, old John Lingle. So, by and by, he heard a deer was coming closer. It was a buck, a big one, and he shot at it, but only crippled it. The deer went for him and he grabbed its horns, and he had the horns like this. And he pinched him in there.

"The deer tried to get him against a tree. And with his hands he turned it around the tree. Now this is no lie. Old John Lingle told me this often. And he said they was coming down the mountain like hell; the dog too. But finally the dog caught them, you know, and the dog jumped up and got him by the throat and choked the deer. Now this is no hot story. Well, he shot him too." [4]

Anyone who thinks the preceding tales are indeed just "hot" stories made up by a hunter trying to impress his hunting camp compatriots should not pass judgment until they've done at least one of three things: spend enough time in the great outdoors to actually get to know the habits of deer, read the autobiographies of the old time Pennsylvania hunters like Philip Tome or Meshach Browing, or talk to some present day hunters and listen to their stories of the mountains.

There is no doubt that bucks will charge a person given the right conditions. Does will too, as anyone who has gotten too close to a doe who is with a new-born fawn can attest, and this writer can be included in that number. In fact, records of several such encounters with the male of the species have been preserved in various historical texts. Histories of Clinton County for example tell of "a citizen who once owned the lands on which Renovo now stands" being charged by a sizeable buck. The account states that the citizen would probably have been gored to death except for the fact that the beams of the horns were so far apart that the man could squeeze himself between them and hold on "so as to not allow the prongs to enter his body". In this case the man "was relieved by the timely arrival of another hunter, who dispatched the buck and rescued him from certain death." [5]

The same historical records of Clinton County preserve another deer-attacks-man story which is said to have occurred near Young Womanstown, Chapman Township. Here some "dogs had closed in upon a buck, but not being able to master him, a workman on the farm undertook to assist the dogs, when he received such a thrust from the buck as to produce a wound in his hand that disabled him for several weeks." [5]

Obviously the stories of hunters' hand-to-hand clashes with deer do include dogs at times, and Philip Tome, the legendary Nimrod of the West Branch Valley and northwestern Pennsylvania, would have had some definite ideas on which breed was best suited to have along in any hand-to-hand, or, more accurately, hand-to-antler, duel with a deer. Tome's fascinating book, entitled *Pioneer Life; or, Thirty Years a Hunter*, preserves his many recollections of the days when he was interpreter for Seneca chiefs Cornplanter and Blacksnake, but it also contains his

181

recollections of the times when he stalked elk, panthers, wolves, and deer in Lycoming, Warren, Potter, and Tioga Counties. His advice to other would-be Nimrods was that to be a successful deer hunter a person "should always procure at any cost, the largest and best dogs to be found," with the best breed being "half bloodhound, a quarter cur, and the other quarter grayhound." [6]

Dogs would, of course, give a serious deer hunter a decided edge, but even then there was always an element of risk. However, despite the dangers that are inherent in deer hunting, there can also be a humorous side. Even Sam Askey, the great "big game" hunter of the Bald Eagle Valley in Centre County, had some lighter moments mixed in with his many "hair-breadth escapes from the wild denizens of the forest." [7] In his later years, Askey was fond of recounting some of his more interesting hunting tales to interested parties, and, since Askey was born in 1776, his stories stretched back to the early 1800's when the mountains of Pennsylvania were a hunter's paradise.

One of Sam Askey's favorite hunting spots was along the old Indian path leading from the Bald Eagle Valley into the small town of Snow Shoe. Known as the Bald Eagle Path, the trail was named after the same local Indian chief whose name rests upon the valley today. It was along this path that Askey had what he would later describe as "an amusing and ridiculous scrape" with a large buck he spotted one day while out hunting. The buck was quite a distance away, but Askey decided to make the long shot anyway, and when his rifle cracked, the deer went down "flat in his tracks". [7]

Thinking he had made a "dead shot", Askey pulled out his hunting knife with his right hand and walked up to the stag. The veteran hunter bent down and grabbed one of the buck's antlers with his left hand, and then started to apply the knife to the bucks' throat. Suddenly, much to Askey's "utter dismay and astonishment", the buck jumped up violently, one of the horns going through part of the oversized shirt that Askey happened to be wearing. "He then gave me a tremendous whirl," recalled the hunter, "in doing which he relieved me of the blouse and departed." Askey was left standing in his shirt-sleeves, relieved to be alive, but amused by the sight of the blouse furling out from the buck's antlers "like the flag of a conquering hero." In later years, when asked if he resented the deer for stealing his shirt, Askey would reply that he did not, noting, "If I had not been relieved of it, the results would have been much more serious." [7]

Despite the historical evidence, deer stories like Sam Askey's, John Lingle's, Jackson Stover's, and other hunter's like them, might still seem far-fetched to those who have never heard these tales of the mountains before. People somehow expect such tales to be exaggerated, since fisherman and hunters have been known to embellish the size of their trophies at times. Moreover, authors like Henry Shoemaker have added their own embellishments to a factual episode now and then, making the authenticity of the entire tale suspect. One example like this might be the deer encounter mentioned in "Hairy John", story VI in this volume. The story of the hog-tied deer waking up and running around the cabin sounds like a touch from the facile pen of Henry Shoemaker, but the episode has become woven into the tapestry of Penns Valley legend and may have been based on real events. Certainly it's obvious that deer can sometimes fight back when desperate. And just in case anyone needs further proof of that, the following tale from Clinton County is offered for the reader's consideration. This incident occurred in the early 1970's on Short Mountain, in the Pine Creek Valley. The area is part of the main chain of the Allegheny Mountains, and lies next to Tiadaghton State Forest near Waterville, gateway to the Pine Creek Gorge and Pennsylvania's Grand Canyon country.

"The one I shot was when I was on a drive, up in Painter Hollow," said Dave Poust, the internationally awarded taxidermist at Waterville. Poust entertained us with many interesting hunting and fishing tales when we visited his taxidermy shop during springtime of 1998, and this tale proved to be one of the funniest.

"It went to jump the run, and all I got was a shot like this [from the hip]. I never got the rifle up. I just took a shot when it was jumping the run. Well, I never figured I'd touched him; He was up there about eighty yards. I went up, and there he laid in the run! Oh boy, big surprise here, you know: I got him!

"I almost kept right on goin' with the drive. There was an old loggin' trail right up from the bank, and I thought, 'Well, I'll just pull him up outa here and put him on that trail, and then when the drive's over I'll come back down and drag him down the main road.'"

"I could see he was hit here in the neck. There was blood here on the neck, and I thought 'Boy, that was a nice shot!' Well, anyway, I put the draggin' rope on him and started to pull him up over the bank, and all at once he's on all four feet! He didn't like bein' led around!

"Well, him and I went around and around in this 'crick' bottom; it's all loose stone and everything, and it was just clangin' and bangin'. I'd set my gun up on the top of the bank first while I got my draggin' rope out. I had him by the end of the rope, and he had me!

"I finally got to a little white pine tree about a little bigger than a broom stick, and I got the rope tied around it. Well, now he's backin' up and he's shakin' his head – it was a big seven point. Nice buck! The other driver that was above me heard all this clangin' and bangin' and he hollered down, 'What's goin' on?'

"I said, 'Come on down!'

"He come down, and I said, 'This one big enough or do you want me to go get a bigger one?'

"He said, 'What's goin' on?'

"I said, ' I didn't know whether to shoot it or let it go!

185

"He said, 'I never seen anything like this!"

"Well, I said, 'If you think it's a keeper, I'll keep it!'

"Here that bullet had just creased the back of the neck, right back of the ears. It never hit the spinal cord or anything. What it did, it knocked it out – the shock through the spinal cord knocked it out. Well, if I'd've kept right on goin', when I come back I'd've sworn somebody stole that deer!" [8]

A Hunter's Camp (circa. 1920's)
East Branch of Big Run, Sproul State Forest, Clinton County
Courtesy Penna. State Archives, Public Relations Office
Photo file #176, RG-6, Dept of Forests and Waters

INDIAN SUMMER

When the first white men set foot in what is now the state of Pennsylvania, they found other people already living here. Christopher Columbus had discovered this race of native Americans on the North American continent at an earlier time, and, thinking he had landed in India, called them Indians. It was an appealing name, and it has endured, but the Indians' culture has not.

The meeting of the white and the native American races at that period of time was a classic confrontation of two civilizations at widely different periods of development. The Indians were still living in the Stone Age in many respects, while the whites had an impressive list of industrial and scientific achievements they could point to with pride. The differences in the cultures were seemingly so great that the whites looked down upon the Indians as primitive savages. On the other hand, what they didn't see was that the Indians had political and social structures of their own that were more just and noble in some respects than many European systems. Moreover, the Indians had an ancient oral tradition that included legends rivaling any that Europe could offer. But once again, in their typically ethnocentric attitude, the whites dismissed the Indians' stories as nothing more than the idolatrous beliefs of a pagan people.

Today, when we read or hear the same quaint tales of the Indian, we aren't as likely to look down upon them the way the first white men to hear them did. The Indian legends, we now realize, preserve a link back to that ancient race of people who were driven from their native lands by another race of men: land thirsty intruders who neither understood the people they were displacing nor wanted to.

This "holier-than-thou" attitude of the white race toward all the native American tribes they encountered led to conflicts: the bloody Indian wars of the 1750's and the 1770's here in the Keystone State. People on the frontier lived in fear during those terrible times — fear of furtive Indian raids led by notorious Indian war chiefs like Shingas, Captain Jacobs, and Hiokoto, and fear of ending up victims of those raids, like so many of their contemporaries. Scalped and dying neighbors were gruesome reminders of the hazards of frontier life, and a night sky reddened by burning settlements over the mountains was another such reminder for the inhabitants of Northumberland County in 1778 and of Lehigh County in 1755.

Gradually the peace-loving Quakers who comprised the Provincial Government in Philadelphia realized they couldn't disregard the plight of the frontiersmen any longer. The Scotch Irish and German settlers needed a means of defense, and so, with great reluctance, the Quakers authorized the construction of a chain of forts that played a key roll in the bloody Indian wars that were to follow. In fact, so effective were these bastions, structures the Indians would later refer to as "strong houses", that they at last provided the relief the white settlers living on the frontier had prayed for. Eventually the frontier forts became such a normal part of the frontier experience that the word "fort" was used as both a noun and a verb.

Raids on pioneer settlements by Indian marauders were always possible during Pennsylvania's frontier days, and no one knew for sure when the sound of the war whoop would be heard in the forest. However, summer was the usual time when roving bands of warriors set out on their bloody mission, and only the most foolhardy or fearless white settlers refused to "fort" during these peak periods when reports of Indian hostilities got too close for comfort. The sturdy log bastions must have looked very inviting during these times of terror, but like almost everything else, there were advantages and disadvantages to living within the relatively safe walls of a fortress.

Inconvenience and discomfort were two drawbacks associated with the "forting" experience. Loss of privacy was another. Being confined in tight quarters with one's neighbors for weeks on end must have been nerve wracking for independent settlers who loved the isolation of the frontier, but the confinement also fostered a sense of cooperation. The natural rhythm of the seasons did not stop just because people were holed up in a fort, and so there was still livestock to feed and crops to tend.

Determined to keep their farms productive even during the times when they were "forted", the agriculturalists of the frontier would occasionally band together and leave the protection of the fortress. Groups of men, their muskets on their shoulders, would make their way back to their clearings, and help one another in their respective fields. Despite the need for as many helping hands as they could get, the fearless farmers always chose one of their number as a sentry to watch for Indians. With the sentry on guard, the others would stack their muskets in a convenient spot and then begin their labors in earnest. However, despite their precautions, settlers like these, with their loaded muskets nearby, were still sometimes killed and captured as they toiled together in their fields.

Given the difficulties of life both inside and outside a fort during times of Indian attack, it is no wonder that frontier families were glad to return to their homes when danger had passed or when the first frosts coated the leaves of sturdy oaks and settled on maples tinged with the first colors of fall. Although their homes were nothing more than crude cabins, they must have felt like castles after the stresses of "forting". Most of us also have pleasant mental pictures of those frontier homesteads surrounded by wide open spaces and verdant forests, but life in those early cabins could be very different than the romantic images we see in our minds today.

"This house looks and smells like a shambles," wrote Rev. Philip Fithian in his journal in 1775. The itinerant minister had been invited to stay with a Centre County settler's family for a while, but the preacher was totally unprepared for the life style of a typical frontiersman. Although he was grateful for shelter, Fithian was appalled by a house filled with "raw flesh and blood, fish and deer, flesh and blood in every part, mangled wasting flesh on every shelf. Hounds licking up the blood from the floor; an open-hearted landlady; naked Indians and children; ten hundred thousand flies", and, he feared, "as many fleas". It was not a lifestyle for a person used to more refined surroundings, and, concluded Fithian, "I would not live here for five hundred a year" [1]

The Indians Fithian mentions were friendly ones, but many were not. It is from this fact that still another term arose from the frontier experience: the term "Indian Summer". It is a phrase that conjures up pleasant thoughts for us today, but once again the reality forming the basis for the expression is far different from our romanticized concepts.

The mention of "Indian Summer" was a sound of alarm to the state's early settlers according to Joseph Doddridge, that early chronicler of western Pennsylvania's Indian wars. [2] Although the first signs of frost meant that Indian war parties would be heading back to their homes in the north, there was always the chance that the icy gusts of November would be broken by a string of balmy days when a smoke-like haze covers the land

191

and the warriors would decide they had time for one more raid before the bone-chilling days of winter arrived at last. The name "Indian summer" was the title the early settlers gave to this season, and it was so appropriate that it became a part of the folklore of the frontier.

Although the expression is rooted in terror, it is such a powerfully attractive one that we still use it today. Perhaps it reminds of a time and place that seems better than it really was; or perhaps we find it appealing because it preserves a memory of a race of people that were wronged, and we feel a need to rectify that injustice. Either way, the expression does evoke images of a vanished people, and so it seemed fitting to discuss its origins in this little essay in order to lay the foundations for two tales that preserve a memory of how the state's Indians eventually became reluctant participants in the white man's culture. The first of these two stories might be called "The tale of the sputtering candles"; the second, "A full-blooded Indian".

The tale of the spluttering candles occurred in a secluded vale near present-day Port Matilda, Centre County, where Laurel Run winds its way down to Bald Eagle Creek. Natives to that area have often seen the highway marker here noting "Reese Hollow Road", just off Route 220 and near the little town whose name poses a bit of a mystery to those who study the origins of such things. On the other hand, although the source of Port Matilda's name has been lost over time, the origin of the name of Reese Hollow is well known to the descendants of John Christian Reese.

"He was a Hessian soldier, brought over to fight, put down the uprising of the colonies, for King George of England," recalled one of Reese's proud descendants. "He got captured at Trenton, New Jersey, when George Washington crossed the Delaware; and then he served two 'hitches' in the navy for George Washington. But it was his granddaughter, which was my great grandmother, that told this story. I knew my great grandmother, but I don't think she told me the story. I think my mother told me the story. My grandmother raised my mother instead of her mother, so it was almost like her mother.

"My great grandmother's name was Delilah. I couldn't tell you when she was born, but my mother was born in 1898. When my great grandmother went to housekeeping she went to housekeeping in a log house, probably with a dirt floor, up in Reese Hollow. There might be stones there from the foundation, but then later on they built a regular house, and it still stands today. John Christian Reese had this whole hollow. He was a millwright, and he had a sawmill there at Laurel Run. They didn't have money to pay [for the land], but some way or other he got it. I don't know, maybe from the war or something. [The Colonial Government didn't have money either, and so often paid the veterans of the Revolutionary War with land grants].

It was here at their homestead, in the hollow that today stills bears their name, that the Reeses were often visited by the last remaining Indians of the area. The visits usually took place without incident, but during one particular time something so unusual happened that it became a treasured part of the Reese family's oral history, and remains so today.

"It was late in the evening, and the Indians came in to get milk for the babies," recalled the man who had heard the tale from his mother. "They would usually give them milk, if they had extra. This one evening they happened by; they wouldn't come regular, I guess. This evening the men were either out hunting or away some place, but the women and the children were there, and [my great grandmother] was one of them.

"And they come in to get milk for their babies, and they'd always give 'em the best they could. But they was always afraid what they'd do when the men wasn't there. And this night the men wasn't there, and they were a little skeptical about what the Indians would be up to.

"But anyway, they had candlelight – it's what they used to see by. And they way they'd do it, they'd dip it into tallow. Then they'd put it over into the water to cool it; and back and forth until they got the candle, the wick, big enough. But then this night they had lit the candles, and it got down to where there must've been some water in it, and it started to spit. And this spitting scared the Indians, and they took off even without the milk for their babies. They was much relieved; they didn't know what the Indians would do!" [3]

The second episode that recalls the manner in which Indians may have gradually learned the white man's ways is a humorous story that once circulated in and around Johnstown, probably about 1890 to 1900. The anecdote may be based on a real incident, or, at the very least, a real Indian, but, at this late date, there is no way to know for sure. However, there are, perhaps, some elements to the story that convey a picture of just how completely many Pennsylvania Indians became assimilated into white society. Whether that assimilation was good or bad can be the subject of lengthy discussions, but there is little doubt that how it all took place is not something that we should look back upon today with a sense of satisfaction or pride.

"The only Indian I ever knew was Sammy Sanook. He was educated at the Carlisle Indian School," recalled the former native of Johnstown. This grand old man was an invaluable link with the past. He had helped with the clean up of the city after Johnstown was devastated by the famous flood of May 31, 1889, and he was two years past the century mark when he sat down with me and talked of the old days. Stories of wolves, ghosts and Indians were common when he was a young man, and his recollection of the Carlisle Indian reminded him of a joke he'd heard when he was fifteen to twenty; a joke about a different Indian who lived somewhere "up around Johnstown".

"This Indian had to pass through town to get to his cabin," continued the man born in the first decade following the Civil War. "On this one day when he was passing through, he saw a blood bank set up there. He spoke good English and so he knew what a sand bank and an ore bank were, but this was new to him.

" So he asked someone, 'Whose blood are they taking now ?' They persuaded him to go have a look, so he did. The nurse there tried to get him to donate, but he was scared. She explained it all to him and showed him that none of the donors had been hurt. So this Indian finally gave a pint and sat down to rest.

"Three white donors finally noticed him sitting there and, since Indians were scarce, asked him if he was a full-blooded Indian. 'Yes,' he said, 'short one pint'. [4]

Today in Pennsylvania's cities there are no easily-identified lone Indians that can be singled out as living reminders of the once-proud and powerful race which at one time lived on this very same soil and hunted in the forests that covered it. It is a sad fact but the verdant land of the Indian has too often been replaced with white man's landscaping. Where there once were forests and fields there are now housing developments, parking lots, factories, and shopping centers that no one wants or which cannot find businesses to rent their space. But despite what seems sometimes to be our best efforts, there will, hopefully, always be some things that we white men cannot take away from native Americans. Those things are the names that they gave to Pennsylvania's mountains, rivers, valleys, streams, and to their own towns, from which come the names of some of our cities. Perhaps the words of the poet say it best, and in a way the Indians might have said it themselves:

> "Ye say they have all pass'd away,
>> That noble race and brave,
> That their light canoes have vanish'd
>> From off the crested wave;
> That 'mid the forest where they roam'd
>> There rings no hunter's shout;
> But their name is on your waters;
>> Ye may not wash it out.
> Ye say their cone-like cabins,
>> That cluster'd o'er the vale
> Have disappear'd as wither'd leaves
>> Before the autumn gale;
> But their memory liveth on your hills,
>> Their baptism on your shore,
> Your everlasting rivers speak
>> Their dialect of yore." [5]

GYPSY CARAVANS

When deciding which tales rank among the most fascinating annals of Pennsylvania's legendary lore, the stories of that unique race of people known as Gypsies must certainly be considered among the candidates. The old-timers who remember them recall the unusual life-style of the Gypsies, but most often they remember their caravans, gaudily-painted horse drawn wagons, that could often be seen winding their way along the back roads and over the mountains of Pennsylvania as late as the first decades of the twentieth century. Known all over the world as wanderers, Gypsies have always been content to live on the fringes of society, taking on occupations that fit in with their mobile life-styles.

In Europe they were often employed in part-time and seasonal work, and also served as dogcatchers, hangmen, undertakers, and in other similar jobs that no one else really wanted to do. Generally, however, the Gypsy men were known for their talents as musicians, blacksmiths, and horse dealers. The Gypsy women, on the other hand, earned money by providing services that a local populace would never consider supplying: unique things such as fortune-telling and theatrical entertainment. But despite their honest endeavors, the Gypsies were also known for their dishonesty. They had a reputation for thievery and for trickery; and, since they seemed to disdain normal societal structures and were strangers wherever they went, they were always treated as outcasts.

People not only mistrusted Gypsies because of their strange lifestyle and cagey reputations, but also because they were not "locals". They had no roots, and no one knew where they came from. They called themselves "Rom", which, when translated from their own tongue, merely means "man", but the early German settlers here in Pennsylvania preferred instead to call them "Zigeuner", meaning "vagrants". English settlers thought that since the word Gypsy was probably derived from the word Egyptian, the Gypsies must have originated in that country, but those who have studied the matter say their country of origin was India.

Their typically dark complexions, jet-black hair, and bright gaudy clothes could be evidence connecting the Gypsies to India, but these things also made them stand out. Moreover, Gypsy women could sometimes be strikingly beautiful, and they accentuated this beauty by wearing large pieces of colorful ornamental jewelry. Wherever they went the flamboyant Gypsies were noticed, and although they were, no doubt, sometimes the culprits, they were also often wrongly blamed for many misfortunes, thefts, and misdeeds that happened in farms, towns, and villages that they passed through; like the time the water turned to poison on Trimble Hill.

About half-way down the slope of Trimble Hill in Indiana County there was once a watering trough. Here the Gypsies used to camp, attracting customers from the many travelers on the public road. People would stop to have their fortunes told or to see the roadside vagabonds perform, but local farmers began to complain about disruptions to wagon traffic. Matters stood unchanged for awhile until a few of the more disgruntled individuals decided to take matters in hand. So it was that one day a band of gun-toting township men marched out to the Gypsy camp and ordered them to leave the area. The cheery vagrants seemed to accept their fate meekly enough, but later on whenever horses drank water from the watering trough on Trimble Hill they became sick, and some died agonizing deaths.

People didn't have to think too long before concluding that the Gypsies had put a curse upon the spring that supplied the water for the trough. It was obvious to most that since Gypsies could tell fortunes they must also know many of the other "black arts", including ways to poison a perfectly good water source. Others weren't so sure, but most local folks didn't give the Gypsies the benefit of the doubt at all, and so the mysterious wayfarers were tried and convicted *in absentia* by the powers of superstition.

Although the way the band of Gypsies was found guilty in this case would not "hold up" in a court of law, it must still be said that Gypsies as a group were not very concerned about their reputations. They were looked upon with suspicion by many of the reputable country folk, who, themselves, were held as second class citizens by some of the more snobbish city types. Condescendingly referred to as "hill men", "clodhoppers", and "Busch Deutsch" by their city cousins, the upstanding inhabitants of rural Pennsylvania during the last cenutry must have sometimes wondered what their detractors called the Gypsies.

Whatever the names used to describe them, the Gypsies were certainly victims of prejudice. However, in this case there were apparently many instances that strengthened and validated those prejudices, just like an episode that took place around 1920 near the quaint Centre County town of Woodward.

"When I was a kid, a bunch of Gypsies, there were a lot of Gypsies back in those days, used to come in here [to present day Woodward Cave and Camp Ground]," recalled the life-long resident of the area. "Of course, they were people that you gotta watch. They made baskets; the women weaved baskets from willows. There was a lot of willows up along here. I think that's why they parked in here. Then the men would go out and sell these baskets during the daytime. But they were also known as crooks and pickpockets, and I do know that actually they did pickpocket R. Stover, an old gentleman at Woodward.

"A man and a woman, Gypsy, came on to the porch and wanted to sell him baskets. He didn't want them. He said, 'I've all the baskets I need,' but they kept talking to him and talking to him, and in the meantime the lady got a hold of his wallet some way. He never found it out 'til after they were gone. His wallet was missing, and he never did get it back. " [1]

Elderly folks living in other parts of the state could probably add their own stories about the thievery committed by Gypsies, just like some of the older residents living in the shadow of Mount Riansares near the small Nitttany Valley town of Mackeyville, Clinton County.

"Oh, Gypsies every summer," chortled ninety-three year old Cliff Vonada. Known for his infectious laugh and easy sense of humor, the old farmer is the unofficial town historian, and is full of remembrances of the old days. Active and hearty his entire life, Mr. Vonada drove a tractor and plowed all his own fields up until this year when his legs finally "gave out". However, his mind is as fine as it always was, and he relishes the memories of his country life, including stories of how the Gypsies used to camp along Fishing Creek in Mackeyville near where the local Kiwanis Club had built a medical center for local residents. He also recalls a day in the first few years of the 1920's when he was mowing hay with a team of horses and these same Gypsies robbed a neighbor.

"They come through every place [with their horses]," stated Mr. Vonada in 1998. "The little lot that's growed up on this side of the Health Camp to the crick was vacant at one time, and Dr. Dunn left them in and they camped there. All they did was camp and rest awhile. They could tell your fortune! Oh yeah, one would tell your fortune while the other was robbin' ya'! They'd come out here, and I remember one time my dad was helpin' Mr. Sager up here – we neighbored. Farmers all went together and helped each other. I was a kid back then, and Mr. Sager's old dad was right back there in this field and these Gypsies come along and got after him. They took his pocketbook and everything. I saw this. So I run up and I tell dad, and they come down and they caught 'em down here. They got back his pocketbook and stuff back they had stolen."

The townspeople must have been furious over the attempted robbery, but the consensus seemed to be that it was more trouble than it was worth to try to retain the Gypsies and their horses until law enforcement officials arrived. None of the culprits were arrested; instead, said Mr. Vonada, they "just let 'em go!". [2]

Gypsies are not as prevalent, or at least not as obvious, today as they once were. Forty-five years ago they could still be easily picked out at county fairs, but they don't seem to attend them any more – at least you don't notice them. Perhaps they've just learned to blend so well into the fabric of modern times that they are unrecognizable from anyone else. On the other hand, maybe there aren't any Gypsies left at all, the Gypsy of old having faded away into the colors and mists of the past. If so, it would mean that the wish of a World War I doughboy no longer has any meaning.

Joyce Kilmer, the American poet who was once famous for his poem entitled "Trees", was killed in France in 1918 during the World War. One of the wishes he had expressed in a letter to his mother was that if he ever owned a piece of woodland he would erect a sign on it saying that Gypsies would be welcome to camp there. When the state of Pennsylvania set aside twenty-one acres of Bald Eagle State Forest, on Paddy Mountain in Union County, for a Joyce Kilmer State Forest Monument they erected a sign at the entrance. On the sign were the words "Gypsies are welcome to camp here". The sign, as well as the Gypsies that it beckoned, now seem to be gone, a missing part of Pennylvania's colorful past.

Footnote: Apparently Gypsies have not entirely disappeared. Now their caravans are formed by gasoline-powered automobiles instead of colorful horse-drawn carriages, but their reputations have not changed. "They were around here the other summer," notes Mr. Vonada; and they are still up to their old tricks, claims Mr. Vonada's wife, who says the Gypsies were here "putting tar on roofs and driveways". The less-than-honest workmen did the job, but they used vastly inferior materials to do it. "Yeah," said Mr. Vonada, "you still gotta watch 'em, they tell me." [2]

ACKNOWLEDGEMENTS
(And a plea for more stories)

Folktales of the "Good Old Days" cannot be preserved unless there are folks who remember them and are, in turn, willing to share them. I've been fortunate to find many such people over the last thirty years, but there are also those who went "above and beyond" my pleas for stories. These are the people who are inspired as much as I am when hearing the episodes of a bygone age, and they are also the ones whose love for our mountains is as great as mine. It is this common bond, I feel, that has moved them to find others who can tell me more "fireside tales".

Among these exceptional helpers is Jim Maguire, Jr., of *Restless Oaks*, in McElhatten, who has spent many hours showing me around the mountains of Clinton County, and who has put me in touch with some excellent story tellers there. Bill and Pat Tyson of Beech Creek in Clinton County also deserve a lot of thanks for their kind efforts and the time they spent uncovering tales and contacts. All three of these Clinton Countians are dedicated to preserving the heritage of that area, and the results of the assistance they've given to me can be found in several episodes embedded in this volume's stories, including "Hand-to-horn Combat" and "Gypsy Caravans". Future volumes in the *Pennsylvania Fireside Tales* series will contain still more tales that have been preserved as a direct result of help from the Tysons and Jim Maguire.

I would like to thank my son James for all the illustrations used in this book and previous ones; his sketches always add a nice touch. Thanks also must go to those readers who have taken the time to write or phone me with their own stories. Contacts like this are always a pleasant surprise and are greatly appreciated. I'm always ready to pursue another "lead", and so I would be delighted to hear from those who have an old-time tale similar to those found in these volumes – particularly hunting episodes from the 1950's or earlier, since I do need more of these types of anecdotes. My address is 143 Cedar Ridge Drive, Port Matilda, Pa. 16870. Thanks, and I'll be in touch!.

FOOTNOTES TO THE TALES

I. Red Panther
    1. Stover, Ray (born: 7/10/1912), recorded 5/19/89
    2. Fletcher, S. W.,
        Pennsylvania Agriculture and Country Life, 1640-1840, 504
    3. Tantaquidgeon, Gladys, *Folk Medicine of the Delaware,* 22
    4. Cornplanter, Jesse J., *Legends of the Longhouse,* 183

II. Wolf Days in Centre County
    1. Linn, John Blair, *History of Centre & Clinton Counties, 571*
    2. Steiger, Randall (born: 1904), recorded 5/4/88
    3. Wert, John (born: 12/22/1912), interview 7/5/81, recorded 2/13/88
    4. Harting, James E., *Extinct British Animals,* 194

III. The Lost Treasure of Penns Creek
    1. Fiske, John, *Myths and Myth-Makers, 54*
    2. Meyer, Dorothy, letter to the author, dated 1978
    3. Brendle, Thomas R., and Troxell, William S.,
        "Pennsylvania German Folk Tales, Legends,
        Once-upon-a-time Stories, Maxims, and Sayings",
        Proceedings of the Pennsylvania German Society – Vol. L., 58
    4. Brendle, Thomas R., and Troxell, William S., *ibid.,* 48
    5. Brendle, Thomas R., and Troxell, William S., *ibid., 46,49,53*

IV. The Tell-tale Tombstone
    1. Brown, Becki, "Ballad of Millheim Cemetery", appeared in
        The Millheim Journal (Donald Heggenstaller, editor), 10/26/72
    2. Heggenstaller, Donald (born: 6/19/1936), recorded 11/18/88
    3. Voneida, Jean (born: 8/31/1934), recorded 11/13/82
    4. Fletcher, Stevenson W.
        Pennsylvania Agriculture and Country Life, 1640-1840, 179
    5. Meyer, Dorothy (born: ??????), interviewed 11/24/72
    6. Glimm, James Y., *Flatlanders and Ridgerunners,* 123
    7. Beers, J. H. & Co.,
        Commemorative Biographical Record of Central Pennsylvania, 337

Pennsylvania Fireside Tales III

V. Taking Fire From a Gun
 1. Brendle, Thomas R., and Troxell, William S.,
    "Pennsylvania German Folk Tales, Legends,
    Once-upon-a-time Stories, Maxims, and Sayings",
    Proceedings of the Pennsylvania German Society – Vol. L., 58
 2. Dyke, Samuel E., *The Pennsylvania Rifle*, 13
 3. Ripka, Jared B. (born: 1885), interviewed 8/27/71 & 2/2/74
 4. Brown, Harry Jr. (born: 1926), recorded 5/21/89
 5. Steiger, Randall (born: 1904), recorded 5/4/88
 6. Musser, Clarence (born: 5/12/1884), interviewed 8/28 & 11/21/71
 7. Brendle, Thomas R., and Troxell, William S., *op. cit.*, 201
 8. Hohman, John George, *POW-WOWS*, 62
 9. Auman, Clayton (born: 10/18/1885), recorded 10/31/81

VI. Hairy John
 1. Krape, Rachael (born: 6/15/1902), recorded 6/23/90
 2. Voneida, Jean (born: 8/31/1934), recorded 11/13/82
 3. Musser, Clarence (born: 5/12/1884), interviewed 8/28 & 11/21/71
 4. Burd, Harry (born: 1905), recorded 5/27/88
 5. Meyer, Dorothy (born: ??????), taken from letter sent to me dated 5/4/78,
    and phone conversation notes of 10/25/80
 6. Manchester, Hugh (born: 10/3/1925), recorded 11/6/81
 7. Fryer, Mr. & Mrs. Jake, recorded 9/13/97

VII. Tooth and Claw
 1. McKnight, W. J.,
    Pioneer Outline History of Northwestern Pennsylvania, 174
 2. Linn, John Blair,
    History of Centre And Clinton Counties, Pennsylvania, 422 ff
 3. Blackman, Emily C.,
    History of Susquehanna County, Pennsylvania, 151
 4. Heggenstaller, Howard (born: 1920), recorded 11/16/89
 5. Stover, Ray (born: 7/10/1912), recorded 5/19/89
 6. Blackman, Emily C., *op. cit.*, 105

VIII. Guardian of the Trail
 1. Montgomery, Thomas L., editor,
    Frontier Forts of Pennsylvania – Vol. I, p. vii.
 2. Sipe, C. Hale, *The Indian Chiefs of Pennsylvania*, 60
 3. Faris, John T., *Seeing Pennsylvania*, 261
 4. Sipe, C. Hale, *op. cit.*, 145
 5. Meginness, J. F., *Otzinachson*, 127
 6. Wallace, Paul, *Indian Paths of Pennsylvania*, 46
 7. Wallace, Paul, *ibid.*, 47
 8. Wallace, Paul, *ibid.*, 48

9. Heggenstaller, Howard (born: 1920), recorded 11/16/89
10. Wallace, Paul, *op. cit.,* 4
11. Ecenbarger, W., "Penn's Sylvania", *APPRISE magazine, 4/89*
12. Henretta, J. E., *Kane and the Upper Allegheny,* 106

IX. Thar's Gold in Them Thar Hills
 1. Sipe, C. Hale, *The Indian Chiefs of Pennsylvania,* 108
 2. Heggenstaller, Howard (born: 1920), recorded 11/16/89
 3. Henretta, J. E., *Kane and the Upper Allegheny,* 156
 4. Stephens, Jim (born: 1924), recorded 12/23/89
 5. Schneck, Rev. B. S., *The Burning of Chambersburg, Pa.,* 33
 6. Author unknown, "Lost Treasure Tales Include Danville",
    appeared in *The Daily Item* newspaper of Danville (unknown date).

X. Campbell's Ledge
 1. Wallace, Paul, *Indians in Pennsylvania,* 160
 2. Davis, Ken (born: 6/19/37), recorded 2/11/90
 3. Jones, W. G. (born: 1905), interviewed 2/2/74
 4. Day, Sherman,
    Historical Collections of the State of Pennsylvania, 432
 5. Peck, George
    Wyoming: History, Stirring Incidents, & Romantic Adventures, 348

XI. Cast Into Stone
 1. "Ancient Legend About Indian Sentry on Caledonia Mountain"; article
    published in *The Gettysburg Times,* 12/27/75 was reprinted from an
    article which originally appeared 8/21/1900 in *The Gettysburg Compiler.*
 2. Stephens, Jim (born: 1924), recorded 12/23/89
 3. Sipe, C. Hale, *The Indian Wars of Pennsylvania,* 743
 4. Heckewelder, Rev. John, *History of the Indian Nations,* 106, 177
 5. Cornplanter, Jesse J., *Legends of the Longhouse,* 86

XII. The Enchanted Bullet Hole
 1. Coco, Gregory A., *On the Bloodstained Field,* 32
 2. Sheads, Col. Jacob M. (born: 4/17/1910), recorded 7/28/89
 3. Kerlin, W. W., *Centre Hall, Centre County, Penna.,* 34
 4. Leckie, Robert, *The Wars of America,* 496
 5. Nesbitt, Mark, recorded 8/28/88
 6. Copied from the letter on display at the Jennie Wade House
    Baltimore Street, Gettysburg (used by permission).

XIII. Fiddling Phantoms
 1. Swetnam, George, "The Fiddling Ghost of Mahoning Valley",
    article which appeared in *The Pittsburgh Press,* 10/30/55
 2. Bayard, Samuel P., *Hill Country Tunes,* pp. 56, 66

3. Faris, John T., *Seeing Pennsylvania*, 193
4. Faris, John T., *ibid.*, 194
5. Wilkinson, Norman B., "Ole Bull's New Norway", *Historic Pennsylvania Leaflet No. 14*, p. 4
6. Lloyd, Thomas W., *OLE BULL In Pennsylvania*, 38
7. Gates, James (born: 7/22/1905), interviewed 9/27/78
8. Faris, John T., *op. cit.*, 194
9. Wilkinson, Norman B., *op. cit.*, 3
10. "You've Got A Ghost In Pennsylvania", Fall Press Release of the Pennsylvania Bureau of Travel Development, date unknown
11. Ingram, John H., *Haunted Homes and Family Traditions of Great Britain*, 4
12. Lockhart, Robert (born: 5/17/32), recorded 12/28/97

XIV. Night Screams
1. Brackett, Luke, recorded 7/19/97
2. Fiedel, Dorothy, recorded 1/30/98
3. Fiedel, Dorothy, *Ghosts and Other Mysteries*, 25

XV. Hand to Horn Combat
1. Bartges, Paul, interviewed 8/28/72
2. Bair, Rev. Lawrence (born: 7/12/20), recorded 11/2/89
3. Malone, Blaine (born: 1903), interviewed 10/23/80 & 4/21/81
4. Auman, Clayton (born: 10/18/1885), recorded 10/31/81
5. Linn, John Blair, *History of Centre and Clinton Counties*, 585
6. Tome, Philip, *Pioneer Life or Thirty Years a Hunter*, 107
7. Linn, John Blair, *op. cit.*, 422
8. Poust, Dave (born: 1930), recorded 2/27/98

XVI. Indian Summer
1. Linn, John Blair, *History of Centre and Clinton Counties*, 16
2. Sipe, C. Hale, *The Indian Chiefs of Pennsylvania*, 13
3. Blazosky, John (born: 8/21/1926), recorded 10/18/96
4. Maurer, Abraham Lincoln (born: 8/6/1872), interviewed 5/25/74
5. Fisher, Sydney G., *The Making of Pennsylvania*, 176

XVII. Gypsy Caravans
1. Stover, Ray (born: 7/10/12), recorded 5/19/89
2. Vonada, Cliff (born: 8/23/05), and his wife Vera, recorded 4/13/98

BIBLIOGRAPHY

Bayard, Samuel P., *Hill Country Tunes*
    Instrumental Folk Music of Southwestern Pennsylvania
    Memoirs of the American Folklore Society - # 39,
    Philadelphia, American Folklore Society, 1944

Beers, J. H. & Co.,
    Commemorative Biographical Record of Central Pennsylvania,
    Chicago, Ill., 1898

Blackman, Emily C., *History of Susquehanna County, Pennsylvania*
    Philadelphia, Pa., Claxton, Remsen & Haffelfinger, 1873

Brendle, Thomas R., and Troxell, William S.,
    `Pennsylvania German Folk Tales, Legends,
    Once-a-upon-a-time Stories, Maxims, and Sayings`,
    Proceedings of the Pennsylvania German Society, Vol. L,
    Norristown, Pa., Pennsylvania German Society, 1944

Coco, Gregory, *On the Bloodstained Field*
    Gettysburg, Pa., Thomas Publications, 1987

Cornplanter, Jesse J., *Legends of the Longhouse*
    Port Washington, N. Y., Ira J. Friedman, 1963

Day, Sherman,
    Historical Collections of the State of Pennsylvania,
    Port Washington, N. Y., Ira J. Friedman, 1843

Dyke, Samuel E., *The Pennsylvania Rifle*
    Lancaster County Bicentennial Committee, 1974

Eckenbarger, William, "Penn's Sylvania",
    APPRISE magazine, Hershey, Pa., April, 1989
    Publication of WITF public broadcasting television

Faris, John T., *Seeing Pennsylvania,*
    Philadelphia, J. B. Lippincott, 1919

Fiedel, Dorothy Burtz, *Ghosts and Other Mysteries*
Ephrata, Pa., Science Press, 1997

Fisher, Sydney G., *The Making of Pennsylvania,*
Published in 1896, reprinted 1969 by Ira J. Friedman, Inc,
Port Washington, L. I., New York

Fiske, John, *Myths and Myth-makers*
(Old Tales and Superstitions Interpreted by Comparative Mythology)
Boston, Mass., Houghton, Mifflin & Co., 1893

Fletcher, Stevenson W.,
Pennsylvania Agriculture & Country Life, 1640-1840,
Harrisburg, Pennsylvania Historical and Museum Commission, 1971

Glimm, James York, *Flatlanders and Ridgerunners,*
Pittsburgh, University of Pittsburgh Press, 1983

Harting, James E., *Extinct British Animals,*
London, Trubner & Co., 1880

Heckewelder, Rev. John,
History, Manner, & Customs of the Indian Nations,
Philadelphia, Lippincott's Press, 1876

Henretta, J. E., *Kane and the Upper Allegheny,*
Philadelphia, Winston & Co., 1929

Hohman, John G.,
Pow-wows, or The Long Lost Friend,
(A Collection of Mysterious Arts and Remedies for Man as Well as
Animals), originally published in the United States in the first decades
of the nineteenth century (approximately 1820).

Ingram, John H., *The Haunted Homes and Family Traditions of Great Britain,*
London, 1905

Kerlin, W. H., *Centre Hall, Centre County, Pennsylvania*
Centre Hall, Centre Hall Fire Company, 1942

Leckie, Robert, *The Wars of America,*
New York, Harper and Row, 1968

Linn, John Blair, *History of Centre and Clinton Counties, Pennsylvania,*
Philadelphia, Louis H Everts Co., 1883

Lloyd, Thomas W., *OLE BULL in Pennsylvania*
Altoona, Pa., Tribune Press, 1921

McKnight, William J., *Pioneer Outline History of Northwestern Pennsylvania,*
Philadelphia, Lippincott Co., 1905

Meginess, John F., *Otzinachson, A History of the West Branch Valley,*
Williamsport, Pa., Gazette Printing House, 1889

Montgomery, Thomas L., editor, *Frontier Forts of Pennsylvania,*
Harrisburg, Pa., Pennsylvania Historical Commission, 1916

Peck, George, D. D.,
Wyoming; Its History, Stirring Incidents, and Romantic Adventures
New York, N. Y., Harper & Brothers, 1858

Schneck, Rev. B. S., *The Burning of Chambersburg, Pennsylvania,*
Philadelphia, Lindsay and Blakiston, 1864

Sipe, C. Hale, *The Indian Chiefs of Pennsylvania,*
Butler, Pa., Ziegler Printing Co., 1927

Sipe, C. Hale, *The Indian Wars of Pennsylvania,*
Harrisburg, Pa., The Telegraph Press, 1931

Tantaquidgeon, Gladys, *Folk Medicine of the Delaware,*
Harrisburg, Pa., Pennsylvania Historical Commission, 1972

Tome, Phillip, *Pioneer Life, or Thirty Years a Hunter,*
Baltimore, Md., Gateway Press, 1989, reprint of the 1854 edition.

Wallace, Paul W., *Indians In Pennsylvania,*
Harrisburg, Pennsylvania Historical Commission, 1970

Wallace, Paul W., *Indian Paths of Pennsylvania,*
Harrisburg, Pennsylvania Historical Commission, 1971

Wilkinson, Norman B., *Ole Bull's New Norway,*
Historic Pennsylvania Leaflet No. 14,
Harrisburg, Pennsylvania Historical and Museum Commission, 1962